Your How-To Guide to

REAL ESTATE
INVESTING

Your How-To Guide to

REAL ESTATE
INVESTING

**LIFE LESSONS ON HACKING YOUR MIND
BEFORE YOU HACK YOUR WALLET**

ALI BOONE

ISBN: 9780578556390
Library of Congress Control Number: 2020907684

The publisher and the author do not make any guarantee or other promise as to any results that may be obtained from using the content of this book. You should never make any investment decision without first consulting with your own financial advisor and conducting your own research and due diligence. To the maximum extent permitted by law, the author disclaims any and all liability in the event any information, commentary, analysis, opinions, advice and/or recommendations contained in this book prove to be inaccurate, incomplete or unreliable, or result in any investment or other losses.

Contents

Preface

I have to admit, writing my first book was both exciting and nerve-wracking. I was eager to get this information out into the world when someone suggested I do it, but I also had no idea what goes into writing an actual book. I've been a writer for a number of years, but mostly for blogs and smaller placements. Writing a whole book proved to be a whole new animal! What was exciting about it though was how much it allowed me to clarify what it was that I really wanted to tell the world. What were the most important things I could tell someone about my real estate investing journey so that they may be inspired and encouraged, and what were the key tidbits I could offer to someone to help them start their own investing journey?

For me to figure out the answers to these questions, I had to really look back and see what things I learned over the years that had the biggest impact on my life and on my investing.

When I sat back and looked for the critical turning points in my real estate investing career, I realized they all revolved around mindset rather than learning about any of the specific investment strategies. This realization was huge. I then went to Amazon to see what books in the real estate investing genre were offering. I found that most of them focused on how-to guides for the various strategies. Did that mean I was unique in that my greatest learnings came from the mindset shifts I was taught rather than the how-to guides? If all of the books out there focused on the how-to guides, that must be what people are reading, and so that must be where they get their biggest learnings.

Was this true though?

There's no doubt that what I care about with real estate investing is probably different than what a lot of other investors care about. I care about real estate investing as a vehicle, rather than a goal. If I only read how-to guides, I'm only learning about how to invest in real estate. But what does that get me, other than an investment property?

Thanks to real estate investing, I'm an entrepreneur who sets her own hours, can travel whenever she wants, live wherever she wants, and gets to create her life in the exact way she wants it. None of those things are in any of those how-to guides on Amazon. That told me that there might be some information missing from Amazon that other investors could benefit from. This kick-started my motivation to pump out this book.

I realize that reading a book about mindset when you're trying to get into something like real estate investing can be frustrating. Chances are if you want to invest in real estate, you want to pull the trigger on your first deal as fast as you can. Trust me—been there. You probably want that how-to guide so you can get into that deal and start your career as an investor as quickly and efficiently as possible.

But what if all it took to create your dream investment portfolio was reading this book?

Okay, chances are it won't be just this book that changes the way you do things. It's going to be a lot of books, a lot of going down Google rabbit holes, and a lot of trial-and-error that gives you all the answers you want. But what is important is realizing that a how-to guide by itself isn't going to get you there.

As you read this book, you will hear me repeat a lot of concepts in different contexts. If I'm repeating something, it's because it's either an extremely crucial concept, or it's a concept that has been vital to my personal journey. It'll also be obvious how I like to invest. It's important for you to know that the critical things on my journey and my strategy preferences may not be fitting for your journey, and that's okay. Every investor's journey is going to be different. What's more essential for you as you read this book is to use it as a means of helping you to figure out your best strategy. Whether that strategy looks at all like mine or not doesn't matter as much as you having the information available to you to help you determine what's a fit for you and what isn't.

I have no doubt that my investing journey looks very different than a lot of people's. But it's worked. I left my corporate job, structured my life in exactly the way I wanted it, and I couldn't be happier. Because I'm sure other people want this as well, I'm sharing the critical things I learned along the way that helped get me here. The only thing that could make me happier now is knowing that sharing what I've learned helped someone else to do the same as I did in using real estate investing as a vehicle for creating their dream life.

As George Bernard Shaw said, "Those who cannot change their minds cannot change anything." It's my hope that by changing your mindset, you'll be able to change your life in exactly the way you want it.

And with that, let's get to mindset hacking.

Ali Boone
Los Angeles, CA
June 2020

Introduction

When I first started thinking about writing this book, the word 'hack' kept coming into my head. I used to be an engineer so I love that word. Like most people, I knew what it meant in the context of 'hacking something', but I decided to throw it into Google anyway. The first thing that popped into my browser screen was:

> To **hack** is to cut or chop something with short, strong blows, like if you **hack** your way through a thick jungle with a machete.
> —Vocabulary.com

Hack your way through a thick jungle with a machete... YES! The real estate investing world absolutely is a thick jungle. It's hard to see through, there are paths going in every direction, there are a few scary creatures, and if you accidentally take the wrong path when nightfall hits, you might be in for a frightful night.

Is it possible to hack the real estate investing industry? Absolutely. But before you can hack an entire industry, there's something way more important you have to hack, and that is *you*. It's about hacking *your mindset*.

When you're willing to hack your mindset, the world is at your fingertips and you can make anything happen. Hacking your mindset is a necessary prerequisite to success. There's not a how-to guide in the world that will help you if you don't have the correct mindset going into it. And, unfortunately with real estate investing, most of us don't start out with the right mindset.

1

Hacking your mindset is ultimately what will allow you to succeed as a real estate investor, to join the investing path that will be most successful for *you,* and to ultimately take control of your life. Hacking your mindset is really essential in all aspects of your life, not just in real estate investing. We have to break the molds from what we've been taught and adjust our thoughts to support what it is we want to achieve.

What has made me successful will not be exactly the same for you. The reason why every single successful person on this planet has made it to where they have is because they found what was right *for them.* Usually, this requires picking out bits and pieces from different ideas and strategies and combining them with your own personal strengths to create something as unique as you are. This is part of the hacking.

That's why I can't do it for you. Your job in reading this book is to take what I give you and figure out if it resonates with you. If it does, figure out how to apply it in creating your own investing success. Maybe you take only one thing away from it or maybe you take all of it or none of it, but either way, the first step in figuring out where you want to go is to explore what's out there.

Some of the ideas in this book are ideas that have existed for a long time but aren't covered in most books. Other ideas are more common concepts that I may just explain a little differently from what you've heard before. Sometimes we just need to hear something at the right time, even if we've heard it before, or in a particular way for us to soar toward success.

I believe there are more perspectives to life, and to real estate investing, than what you'll find floating around on the internet. In fact, if you research real estate investing and how best to do it, you're likely to find that the majority of what you read will conflict with what I'm about to tell you. And to that I say—cool. If you like doing things the hard way and keeping a certain level of work and stress over your head, who am I to argue? I just prefer to do things a different way and that's what I intend to show you throughout this book. I intend to show you a new mindset about real estate investing, and I hope these concepts will expand your ideas in other areas of your life as well.

How I Got Out of the Corporate World and into Real Estate Investing

I think it's important to tell you my story and explain how I got into real estate investing. Through the years, I've come to believe that hearing other people's stories can be extremely powerful for inspiration, motivation, and direction. I'm also not a huge fan of reinventing the wheel, so if I can learn from other people's experiences and mistakes, I assume it will save me time and stress not having to figure it all out on my own.

The very first day I started my corporate job as an aerospace engineer, I knew I wanted out. I had been working as a flight instructor while finishing a Master's degree at Georgia Tech. Compared to my adventures in flight instructing, walking into a secluded cubicle felt a bit… drab. With no exaggeration, it felt like my soul got sucked out through my toes the instant I walked into that cubicle. I also couldn't stand the professionally-ironed business casual outfit I was wearing, and I most certainly wasn't a fan of what time the alarm clock had gone off that morning. I immediately flashed back to when I was 13, sitting in math class solving math problems faster than the teacher could dish them out, thinking about how I wanted to be my own boss and make a lot of money. I probably hadn't thought of that moment since I was 13, but it came flying at me as I stared into that cubicle. This was looking like the opposite of being my own boss. I figured though that since I had just spent so many years in school to get to that cubicle, I should exercise some patience and give it a shot.

I gave it a shot for five years. I can confidently say I spent way more of that time trying to figure out how to get out of my corporate job than I actually spent *on* my corporate job. I was finally able to jump the corporate ship toward the end of those five years. It may seem like a short amount of time, but I can tell you that those five years were full of more researching and trying and failing than you could ever imagine, all in attempt to find my way out. I had no idea how I was going to get out of corporate, and there were no obvious answers around me. I had only a blank sheet of paper in front of me to formulate my escape plan. All I knew was that the only way to get out of a 9-to-5 job would be to either start a business or do something with real estate, so I bought every business and real estate book I could find.

Fortunately, a friend told me about *Rich Dad Poor Dad* by Robert Kiyosaki. My guess is if you're reading this book, you've probably read it. That book quickly set a precedent for the other books I would read during this research-intense phase of my life. I really resonated with what Kiyosaki was explaining in that book, so I made sure that anything else I read was in support of his teachings. I knew even before I finished the book that my life was about to change. I could literally feel my brain rewiring itself with every page I read. (I still wonder today if the friend who recommended that book to me knows how much of a monster she created by giving it to me.)

I'm not going to spend an inordinate amount of time telling you everything I tried in those five years, every mistake I made, and all of the details of the whole journey. Just know that I dug in like my life depended on it. I was researching both business and real estate. I bought tons of books, which obviously included just about every book in the *Rich Dad* series, I paid for some $495 weekend workshops, and I went to various investment and business networking meetings and conferences.

One of the driving quotes I used during each of those events was, "Fake it 'til you make it." I didn't fake my experience to the point of sounding like an idiot, but I would present myself as having a lot of confidence and education on what I was 'involved with', even if it wasn't completely true. I always acted as if I was already in the industry, whatever the applicable industry was, and I tried to ask intelligent and explorative questions, looking everywhere for useful pieces of information.

While this tactic worked well for getting started, I eventually caught myself spinning my tires and not moving forward. I realized this was because I was researching too many things. It was time to pick—business or real estate? I chose business. It seemed like a faster way to build a salary and it could be done with less capital. Then I thought—*what business do I start?* The only thing I could come up with was buying and running a self-storage facility because my family had previously owned self-storage facilities, so I immediately signed up for the annual self-storage convention in Las Vegas. I showed up intending to get every piece of information I could on self-storages. Then I'd figure out how to buy one.

Less than two weeks after returning home from the conference, I received a random advertisement for a real estate investing opportunity in my inbox at work. (I had signed up for every mailing list possible so I'd have a maximum amount of emails to tend to in an attempt to avoid doing actual work.) It seemed like an innocent webinar, so I signed up, watched it, and the next thing I knew I was sitting in front of one of the consultants on the project and later slapping a decent amount of cash down on this investment. And to make the story a little more entertaining, this was no run of the mill investment. I bought into a pre-construction beach development in Nicaragua. Yes, Nicaragua the 3rd world country. I have always enjoyed doing things that make people raise an eyebrow…

Apparently I was going the real estate investing route instead of the business route.

Knowing this investment would have delayed returns because it was pre-construction, I saw it merely as something smart to do with my money while still working at my corporate job. Not once did I think this was my ticket out of corporate. I quickly found real estate investing to be very addictive. Soon a lot of my focus was on trying to figure out how I could buy more. This completely distracted me from trying to find a way out of my corporate job. I put so much thought and focus into real estate at this point that I ended up buying five properties in a year and a half, primarily using creative financing. I was pretty proud of myself. I also figured out that I loved this real estate thing! I was going on trips dealing with the investments, I was meeting some amazingly cool people, and I was finally able to apply my problem-solving brain to some real action.

I eventually started pulling my focus away from Nicaragua and paying more attention to U.S. rental properties. These properties were unique because they were *turnkey rental properties,* which meant I didn't have to do any of the rehabbing or landlord work on them. People who knew me started getting intrigued about what I was investing in because they saw that I wasn't swinging hammers, I wasn't wholesaling, and I wasn't negotiating deals, all of which seemed to be standard tasks for a real estate investor. Everyone wanted to know how I was investing without doing any of that work.

I began referring people to the investment opportunities I was buying into. Shortly after, I learned that if I got my real estate license, I could earn referral fees for anyone I sent over who purchased a property. So I did, thinking this was going to be some good side money in addition to my corporate paycheck. I hadn't forgotten that I wanted out of corporate, but I was so busy with real estate now that I didn't have time to find a way out of my cubicle.

I began effortlessly sending people to the investment opportunities I was buying into. Eventually, I woke up one morning thinking, *"Wait a minute… If normal real estate agents can make a living, and I make the same as a normal real estate agent (while doing way less work), could I make a living doing this?"*

And there it was—my ticket out of corporate.

Sure, it sounds like it was all easy and greasy, but I can promise you that jumping the corporate ship (whose buffet lines serve Friday paychecks and killer portions of health insurance) was the most humbling thing I've ever done. For someone who's always had control issues, suddenly having no control over anything was quite the experience. I did it though. I suffered and struggled through the beginning years of starting a business, as any entrepreneur has to, and I made it happen. I was on food stamps for the first year of having my own business, and I never knew where my next rent payment was going to come from.

During those first few years, not only was I trying to learn how to build a business, but I was still knee-deep into real estate investing with my own properties. I was writing weekly articles for one of the world's largest real estate investing websites at the time and participating every day in their forums, talking to people about different investment strategies and investor mindsets. I was also working directly with investors who were buying their own properties and helping them through the buying processes. On top of doing all that for the business, I was learning to be an owner for all the properties I had bought for myself. In each of those different areas, I was learning more and more about real estate investing and the mindsets of everyone involved.

And that's how I figured out that people need help. Not only do I know people need help because I talk to so many people who tell me they are trying to figure it out, but I also know that people need help because I know I could've used some when I first started out. For instance, I remember always thinking that owning a rental property was smart. I think I had just heard that growing up, which I'm sure is the same for many other people. In the earlier years of my real estate curiosities, I ran around Orange County, California, with a respected real estate agent looking at potential rental properties for sale. Every property I looked at was a total dumper—one even had a dead rat in it in full rigor mortis—and the cheapest property was $271,000. Each of these properties was expected to only bring in about $1,200 per month in rent. I had no idea how to run numbers on a rental property at that time, but all I could think was that something didn't seem to add up with those numbers (pun intended). Where would the profit be? I couldn't pinpoint what the specific problem was, but I felt like something didn't work, so I didn't buy any of them.

But isn't owning a rental property smart? Yes, but not owning just *any* rental property. One of the most critical things on any property investment, rental property or otherwise, are the numbers. Numbers are what make for a good investment property, and learning how to run them is one of the most important things you need to learn to be successful as a real estate investor. Had I known how to run the numbers on these rental properties, I would've quickly seen why they were all terrible investments. At the time though, I didn't even know I needed to run the numbers, much less know how to do it.

But, before you focus on learning numbers and the intricacies of what makes for a good or bad investment property, you have to first adjust your *mindset*.

This is where I come in. You can certainly stick to the old theories about how to be a real estate investor: learn how to find distressed properties, learn to negotiate deals, learn how to be a landlord, and of course learn rehabbing. You need to swing hammers to be a real estate investor, right? Wrong.

I can tell you I've never once had an interest in *working* for my investments. I've never had an interest in swinging hammers, nor have I ever had the skill. Should I have just forced myself to swing hammers so I could invest in real estate, or should I have just sat out and let the hammer-swingers do their thing? Neither option seemed appealing. I was interested in *investing*, not working. But it seemed like the two went together.

Regardless of how you may or may not want to structure your investing, my point isn't necessarily just to introduce you to how I like to invest but rather to get you thinking about possibilities that you may not know exist when it comes to investing, just as I didn't know about the possibilities.

For example, maybe you don't know what all of your *options* are for your goals. Maybe you don't know that you can be extremely passive with your investments, and that passive income is an option for one of your goals, just as I didn't know when I started out. But now that you're learning about passive income, it may be something you want to add to your list of goals. Then, once you've identified your goals, you can begin exploring different investment strategies to achieve those goals.

I know my story isn't the end-all solution for anyone, but I also know a lot of people are exactly where I was: craving a life of their own. They want to break free of jobs they hate, they want financial security, and they want any knowledge they can find as to how to do that. They want to be themselves, and in today's age, that can be incredibly hard to do.

So I hope my story can ignite the little fire inside of you, widen your view of what's possible, and help you shift your mindset about real estate. The biggest thing I want you to take from my story is that if you really want something and you continue working hard toward it no matter what, the answer will eventually present itself.

I'm going to offer you some perspectives on real estate investing and the psychology behind it. I'm also going to expose some myths about real estate investing. Finally, I'm going to tell you about some things that are required to make it big as an investor.

Before we get started, a little word of caution: if you've somehow read this far and you're still expecting a how-to on more traditional real estate investing strategies, or you want to learn the more technical details of the industry, this is the wrong book for you. This is a book of insights into optional mindsets that you can adapt into your investing strategies. Nothing more. It presents options for hacking your mind so that you may ultimately hack your real estate investing career into being exactly what you want it to be. There's a reason it's called NOT your how-to guide.

On that note, let's start hacking.

part one

What You've (Probably) Never Heard About Real Estate Investing

chapter one

Real Estate Investing: There's No Other Job Like It

R eal estate investing, compared to other industries, has its own unique blend of characteristics, requirements, quirks, and drawbacks. With those individualities comes a distinctive opportunity for reward. Most of the greatest financial success stories in all of history somehow involve real estate investing. But is it necessarily an industry for you?

Choosing any avenue in life involves understanding what you'll be taking on if you choose to go down that route. This chapter explores some qualities of the real estate investing industry that you may or may not be aware of.

There are a million industries out there where you can find a job. There's a college degree for just about everything now. With the advent of the internet, there's really no limit to what trades or businesses you can get involved in. And just like they say with dating, there's something for everyone.

But have you noticed how the workplace and the job market have changed over the years? Getting and keeping a job isn't at all what it used to be. Our grandparents worked more labor-intensive jobs, with little creativity, and college degrees were rare. Then college degrees started becoming more popular and a person's path to the workplace was fairly straightforward—get a degree, and that degree will get you a job in that industry (probably a 9-to-5 job). Then as the Millennials have arrived, it's started to seem like college degrees mean nothing anymore because so many people remain jobless after they finish school. This has created a situation where people now are really having to take their career paths and income potential into their own hands. Following a standard path is no longer a guarantee of job security.

Real estate investing is one of few industries that fit this demand for creativity.

There is no standard job path for real estate investors. You can come from a highly educated background or a minimal education background. You can come from wealthy parents or poor parents. You can be an investor anywhere you want. There's no one right way to be an investor. You can make your investing career whatever you want it to be. You literally get to do whatever you want to do. How many jobs or industries are there where you get to do that?

The creative aspects of being in real estate investing can be seen as either positive or negative. Some of these characteristics will make real estate investing more appealing to you and some might make you run as far as possible in the other direction. At the very least they may give you greater insight into what you can expect as you dive into the real estate investing world.

You Are Your Own Educator

Unless the education system has changed recently, schools don't teach real estate investing. Money and finances, in general, aren't even taught. I learned how to do parallelograms but not my taxes. I can promise that knowing parallelograms is not very helpful every year when I need to file my taxes. So if we didn't even learn how to do our taxes in school, which people have to do every single year of their adult life, we certainly didn't learn anything about investing either.

This is a major hurdle for people looking to get into real estate investing. How are you supposed to learn how to do it? I knew generic information about real estate investing while growing up: own a rental property, buy an apartment complex, flip houses, and rehab houses. All the basics. But I knew nothing about the practical application of the process or how to do any of it successfully. Remember those rental properties I looked at in Orange County? The one with the dead rat in it? How could I have known how to run the numbers on those? When was I ever taught how to do that or even that I needed to do that to evaluate it as an investment? In that position—being a brand new investor with no idea of what I was supposed to be looking for—how could I learn what I needed to know?

Well, I had to figure it out on my own. You'll likely be in the same situation when you start out in real estate investing. Not only will you have to learn about the different ways to be a real estate investor, but you'll also have to figure out how to pursue one of the available options. Moreover, I assume you'll want to learn how to do it *well* and not just learn how to do it any old way, which is a whole other level.

Unlike when I got started in real estate investing, there's the added problem now of TMI: too much information. When I started, I was hard-pressed to find resources to learn all of this stuff. Now, thanks to the internet, there's so much information available it can almost be paralyzing. At a minimum, how do you know what information is legit and what is total bunk? Just because something is written on the internet doesn't make it valid. There's no shortage of forums full of people spouting off information when they actually have no idea what they're talking about.

This might turn you off of real estate investing—having to teach yourself how to do it and being reliant on what you learn to keep you out of trouble. If you aren't that interested in teaching yourself new things, or you don't feel confident in your general initiative skills, real estate investing might prove to be out of your comfort zone and outside of your interest levels. Real estate investing does require a certain initiative and drive that many people don't have.

But if you're like me and love creativity and figuring out how to make things happen, you can thrive while teaching yourself the information. Unlike a lot of jobs where you're taught exactly how to do them, there's really no end to what you can learn in real estate investing. If you're independent, enjoy learning, have at least a little baseline intelligence and are willing to do some creative problem-solving, real estate investing might be fantastic for you.

Formal Education Is Irrelevant

Well, sort of. There are several things you learn in school that can help you in real estate investing. Most of my academic background was in engineering, and I can promise you that my fervent spreadsheet and number-crunching skills have played a huge role in my investing career. However, I know several successful investors who do way more impressive things in real estate than I do, and they have very little formal education.

We live in a day and age, finally, where now we understand that people have different kinds of genius. It used to be that if someone couldn't pass a math class, it was assumed they weren't smart and they got judged as such. We know now though that, for example, genius artists aren't likely going to be able to pass a math class very well, and yet that says nothing about their true intelligence. So not doing well in school is far from an indicator of what you're truly capable of.

In an industry like real estate investing where creativity thrives, those students who didn't necessarily do as well with the book-smart type of learning can not only have plenty of chances to succeed in real estate, but they also stand a potentially greater chance of thriving even more than someone who only has book-smarts.

What you may or may not have accomplished with formal education in the past has no bearing on your potential for success as an investor. Besides, you're rarely ever asked to hand in a resume in this industry, so you don't need to worry about populating the 'Education' section with anything fancy, if anything at all.

Flexibility

It's almost crazy how many different ways there are to be a real estate investor. For example, if you've ever started researching becoming a real estate investor, you've probably seen information on:

- wholesaling
- rental properties
- flipping
- notes
- tax liens
- landlording
- syndications
- REITs
- land purchases
- mobile home investing
- self-storage investing

And that's just to start. The list is endless, and each option involves completely different skillsets, risk levels, effort levels, capital requirements, and strategy. Having so many options often makes it more difficult to find your niche, but the wide range of options really does make it an appealing industry to many. Not only does real estate provide flexibility in what you do, but it's also flexible in *how* you can do things.

Let's say of that list above, you choose flipping as your real estate investment strategy. Within the realm of flipping, there are a million ways you can do it:

- Focus on particular areas or neighborhoods.
- Focus on particular property types.
- Source your properties from various means.
- Do the work yourself or manage contractors.
- Finance the investment with different types of loans.
- Take on only one property at a time, or you can out-source a crew, allowing you to oversee multiple properties at one time.

You can also create a flexible schedule, depending on how you structure your strategy. Maybe you want real estate investing to just be a side gig outside of your day job. In that case, you may just take on smaller projects or focus more on outsourcing the work. Maybe you want real estate investing to be your full-time gig, at which point you'd be tailoring your strategy and approach to be income-focused since you'd be dependent on that single income. You can make your investing a side thing, a part-time job, a full-time job, or any amount of time in between those, but regardless of how much time you decide to dedicate to real estate investing, you can also structure *when* you work those hours. If you're pursuing that flipping deal, maybe you spend 4-6 months doing crunch time on a flip project, but once it's over, you take an entire month off and go travel and relax before starting your next project. Or maybe as you're working on a project, you prefer to sleep in and work later in the day rather than waking up at 6am and starting early like you would at a regular job.

The layers of flexibility in real estate investing are endless. This ties back to what I was saying about figuring out what works best for you and what will allow you to keep your sanity. With so many options for flexibility, there's no reason to strain yourself by doing something you hate, doing it in a way that you hate, or on a schedule that you hate. While there are some tried and true methods for success (and tried and true methods for utter failure, too), there is no official requirement for how you do things.

Some people will actually find this terrifying. Plenty of people need or want structure. There are some ways to be in real estate investing without being reliant on flexibility, but if you're someone who thrives on flexibility and wants to do life your way, real estate investing is a fantastic place to be. I actually can't think of an industry more flexible than real estate investing.

You Can Choose Your Co-Workers

In just about every regular job scenario, you will have to work with other people. You usually don't have much of a say in who those people are. You're likely to have to tolerate someone you don't like, be forced to see that one jerk-off you hate every week in staff meetings, and there's a good chance you might butt heads with your cubicle neighbor. There are endless scenarios in which you won't like one or more of your co-workers. And you really can't control who comes and goes.

It's very different when you're a real estate investor. As an investor, you're the boss of your own experience. You get to make the decisions, you can structure your work how you want to, you can decide how to do things, and you can set your own schedule. You also get to decide who you work with. Unlike in the cubicle, you can choose your co-workers, and you don't necessarily have to be stuck with the same co-workers day in and day out. It's a very fluid environment, and you aren't forced to work with someone you despise. Then, when you find good folks that you like to work with, you can try to keep them on your team on an ongoing basis and maximize your relationship with them. The choice is always yours.

A reality to this, though, is real estate investing is also an industry with a lot of characters (to put it nicely). While you can choose who you work with and who you don't work with, sometimes the best person for a particular job or service is just an asshole. In real estate investing, there are no regulations against how someone has to act or behave or what personality they need to have.

There's even a fair chance one or more of your 'co-workers' could have been engaged in criminal activity somewhere along the line. Somehow, that just comes with the territory. I'm not saying I run into a lot of murderers in real estate, but I've worked with a lot of people who were at some point in trouble for something related to real estate or numbers or money or who-knows-what in the past. I think the reason for this is two-fold: one is that there are so many gray areas in real estate that it's easy to accidentally get caught in one of them and get in trouble, and the other is that real estate investing can attract certain personality traits. Think about it: formal education isn't required, customer service isn't required, creativity is required, and there's always risk involved. A lot of criminals fit perfectly into those categories and skillsets. Plus, there's no requirement for background checks in real estate investing, which works in the favor of shadier characters.

On the positive side, if you've ever desired to be in an industry full of colorful characters, you've found the perfect match with real estate investing! But the point remains—in this industry, you will always have flexibility in who you work with and who you don't work with. Unless you own your own business, I don't know of another job with so much flexibility in that regard.

A Chance to Use Your Backbone

It's not a stretch to say that you will need a backbone in this industry to fend off the not-so-uncommon lack of customer service. It's not that people necessarily have malicious intent with their obnoxious personalities, but it's more that people are moving fast and hard in this industry without a lot of time for pampering. Plus, investing is and will always be about the numbers; it's not about the experience. Newer investors tend to get caught in the misperception that the experience matters when it should really be all about the numbers. When it's all about the numbers, that's what people are focused on, and the experience and the customer service aspects can quickly take a backseat.

If you work a 9–5 job, using your backbone may not always be welcome. In fact, it might actually earn you some enemies. In real estate investing, on the other hand, a backbone is required. You may never have to use it, but it needs to be on standby in case you do. Sometimes things go wrong, and when they do, you have to be ready to put your foot down. If you aren't able to do that, you (and your finances) can be quickly taken advantage of.

In no way does using your backbone require you to scream or freak out at anyone; it simply means you don't let people run over you. You put your foot down when necessary, you make sure what needs to happen happens, and that's that.

If you are timid and scared to stand up to people, real estate investing might not be for you. Plenty of people never have to use their voice depending on how they decide to invest, but you always have to be willing to protect your investment. And even if you never have to use your backbone, at a minimum, you need to be willing to take initiative.

Be Whoever You Want to Be

In most jobs, you have to present yourself in a certain way in the interview and then carry yourself in a certain way in the day-to-day. The expectations for a real estate investor are quite the opposite.

- You don't have to dress a certain way.
- You don't have to report to anyone.
- You can even be one of those assholes I referred to earlier.

For the record, I don't condone the latter. I hate dealing with assholes, and I'm very much of the stance that being nice and respectful to others will always put you farther along the path of success. However, I have known some extremely successful real estate investors who were absolutely miserable to work with.

Asshole or not, because you are your own boss and you're creating your own world as a real estate investor, you can create that world around whoever you want to be. Hopefully, it's not the ability to be an asshole that appeals to you but rather the idea that you really can be yourself; you don't have to change yourself to fit who a corporate manager would prefer you to be.

If you have a great product to sell, that's all investors care about. If you are the investor and you have the money to buy something, it's unlikely anyone is going to turn you down based on your personality or how you present yourself.

Having Control over Effort and Reward

Imagine working on a big job for a big corporation, putting in double-overtime consistently to get a project done and giving it your all. Then, when you're finished, it feels like the project disappears into thin air and you get little to no credit for it. Sound familiar? In real estate investing, the amount of effort you put in is much more likely to result in a proportionate amount of reward. Of course this may have its ups and downs, and it can take some time to see the positive rewards, but with real estate investing you can easily see it. You can claim the credit for your work, and you have the ability to increase the reward levels.

There also tends to be a more direct correlation between risk and reward in real estate investing than in a lot of other industries. In real estate investing: the greater the risk, the greater the (potential for) reward. This also means there's a greater chance of flopping (hence the risk part), but that's why the projected returns are typically higher on higher-risk projects; the higher returns are the projected reward for taking on that higher level of risk.

Within that same spectrum though, you have the flexibility to choose your risk/comfort level. You can invest in the least-risky investments and the highest-risk investments, and you can invest anywhere in between. This is fantastic because anyone can be involved in real estate investing, regardless of where they fall on the risk scale. From the most risk-averse person to the total adrenaline junky—everyone can jump into the real estate pool. The risk-averse person can wear floaties on their arms and the adrenaline junky can go straight for the deep-water dive.

Creativity Is Not Only Encouraged—It's Required

There's no one way to invest in real estate. There are a thousand different ways, and within those, there are at least a hundred different ways to do each of those thousand ways.

Because there's no one way to invest in real estate, an investor is forced to get creative about how to best succeed in any given scenario. So creativity is not only encouraged, it's required. There's one caveat, though: it's not always *you* who has to be creative. Someone has to, but you may be able to meet other contacts who can cover the creativity part for you and you just follow along. Or if you're fortunate enough to find a straightforward how-to guide on exactly how to do some investment strategy, the required creativity on your part may be minimal.

But really, the more creative you allow yourself to be as a real estate investor, the better. If you only ever do what other people tell you to do, you're probably only going to get so far. That's where this industry gets really amazing—you get to piece together the best of everything you learn to create some level of awesomeness for yourself. Maybe it's only me who gets excited about this because my engineering brain loves to put puzzle pieces together, but this is a unique aspect of this industry. There is no restriction on *how* to do something. Well, legally there can be restrictions on how you do the more technical bits of it, but as a whole, there's a lot of room to create your strategy and processes however you want.

If you're the kind of person that likes to be creative, likes putting puzzle pieces together, or enjoys problem-solving, real estate investing may be heaven for you. If you're the kind of person who hates all of those things, your best bet is to team up with people who have procedures laid out or who can take on the creative side for you.

One of the Few Places 'Failure' is So Promising

I hesitate to use the word 'failure' because people think of failure as a disappointment, a letdown, or possibly a catastrophe. Nobody likes failure. But what if I told you there's no such thing as failing? But instead there are only learning opportunities? I'm going to stick to the word *failure* though because it's the word most people know and it's the word that needs redefining.

Failure isn't bad. In fact, it's required. Especially in real estate investing. Think of it this way—have you ever heard of a big-time investor like Bill Gates or Warren Buffett who didn't at some point lose millions of dollars? No, you haven't, because they don't exist. Successful investors (and business owners, athletes, coaches, and experts in any industry) have all experienced failure. The difference between those who succeed and those who don't is that the successful ones get up, brush the dirt off, learn the lessons, and continue toward the goal, whereas the ones who don't succeed let failure take them out. My favorite illustration of this comes from Michael Jordan:

> "I've missed more than 9,000 shots in my career. I've lost almost 300 games. Twenty-six times I've been trusted to take the game-winning shot and missed. I've failed over and over and over again in my life. And that is why I succeed."
>
> —*Michael Jordan*

Like Michael Jordan has done in basketball, the most successful investors have failed to fairly heroic levels. Heroic in the sense that they survived catastrophic losses before they made it big; some even survived more than one catastrophic loss. It's not to say that you have to experience catastrophic loss to succeed in real estate investing, but building your ability to overcome challenges will only help you to succeed to greater levels. You've just got to have the confidence to brush yourself off when you've fallen and get back on the horse.

I lost $40,000 on my very first investment. That was enough money to tempt me to run for the hills and do something safer than real estate. But I kept going. Since that time, I know I've easily made back that $40,000 in other ways. And not just monetarily; real estate investing has changed my life for the better in ways I never could've imagined.

What if I had let losing $40,000 scare me and I had quit? At a minimum, I'd still be working my 9-5 job that I hated. Worse than just hating that job though, I never would have started my business. I wouldn't be my own boss. I wouldn't be living in my dream location. I wouldn't be snowboarding during the week. I wouldn't be making as much money as I do with my business.

And the list goes on. When I look at it in perspective, $40,000 seems like a small price to pay for all of that, no?

Learning real estate investing is like trying to learn calculus before you learn to add. Not only did we not learn how to be a real estate investor in school, but we also weren't taught general fundamentals of money and finances or the logistics of financial strategy as a way to understand the reasons for and importance of investing. So how could you not 'fail'?

Unless you're some kind of rare genius who knows exactly what you're doing right out of the gate and never have to make a mistake to learn, you're going to make mistakes. It's just a part of the game. 'Failure' doesn't say anything about who you are as a person. It doesn't mean you're dumb or you can't make it in the industry; rather, it says you were willing to give it a try, which is more than a lot of people can say. So, really, it says quite the opposite than how bad you suck.

Anytime you begin to feel a sense of failure in your investing career, the first step is to remember that whatever happened doesn't constitute failure. It just means you have something to learn. Real estate investing is an industry where on-the-job training is the norm. You're inevitably going to learn a lot of what you need to know as you go rather than ahead of time. That doesn't negate the need to take the time to learn the basics, but you will still make mistakes along the way. Your job is to learn from those mistakes. Essentially, 'failure' can really be celebrated in real estate investing. It means you tried.

However, if you're absolutely paralyzed by the idea of failure, real estate investing may not be for you. But if you're like me and you like a good challenge, you have the confidence to brush yourself off, and you love sharing hilarious lessons-learned stories over drinks, then real estate investing is definitely the spot for you.

You Can't Get Fired

Another reason real estate investing is such a great place to 'fail' is because you can't get fired. Being an investor is more or less a solo venture and the only person who can fire you is you. Therefore, if getting fired equates to failing for you, then that's one way you can't fail in real estate.

———

Investing in real estate really is like no other job out there. It may not be for the meek of heart, but if you're willing to dive in and experience it, you open up the door to a unique level of potential not found in other industries.

chapter two

Debunking the Myths

Unfortunately, myths run rampant in the world of real estate investing. The internet is so overloaded with people yammering on about what they think they know that it becomes increasingly difficult to discern between who you should and shouldn't listen to. How can you tell the difference between truth and lies on the internet? Sometimes a claim might be true, but how can you know if it's true for your particular situation?

When I started getting into real estate investing, I was hearing a lot of common ideas about what you had to do to be an investor and what made for good investments. I assumed those ideas were facts. As I went along in my investing career and then continued to run my real estate investing business, it became clear to me that many of these weren't actually 'facts'. Now, after years of real estate investing experience, I see that a lot of people believe the same myths I used to believe, and they believe new myths that have surfaced in the years since I started. Hopefully debunking some of these myths will open up a realm of possibilities as you start investing.

Myth: You Have to Swing a Hammer

Any time I ever thought about real estate investing I thought of swinging hammers. Actually I always first thought of fixing toilets, but swinging hammers seemed to be where the real bucks were. I thought I would need to find a distressed property, rehab it, and flip it. Isn't that the standard real estate move? Of course it is. And for good reason—it's a great way to make money. But what I didn't know at the time was that swinging hammers was far from the only way to invest in real estate and make a profit.

I think this is why so many people hesitate to invest in real estate—it seems a bit complicated. Yes? Well maybe it's not why *you've* held off, but it was definitely why I resisted for so long. All I kept hearing was 'find motivated sellers, negotiate deals, rehab a property, find tenants, be a landlord'. Not to sound all dramatic about it, but every time I heard that mantra (that I had made up), I wanted to throw up in my mouth a little. I had literally no interest in doing even one of those things. But if it was the only way to invest in real estate, I suppose I'd have done it. After all, those things can be hugely profitable, **but it's not the only way to make a buck in real estate.** If you try to do all of those things and they don't come naturally to you, or you hate them, swimming upstream won't do you any favors for profits down the road. Even if you make the profit later, completely losing your sanity along the way may not be worth it.

There are plenty of ways to invest in real estate without having to swing a hammer. The most basic way would be to invest in real estate notes or in real estate investment trusts (REITs). These approaches are similar to investing in stocks—you just buy the note or invest in the trust and then you're mostly hands-off. Another way, if you want to own real property, is to do like I do and buy rent-ready/turnkey rental properties and hire a property manager to oversee the property on your behalf. The property is ready to rent, or already rented, and it's already rehabbed. Then instead of you landlording the property yourself, you turn the tasks over to a property manager who manages the property for you. At that point, your only job is to just keep an eye on the property and the manager to ensure they are performing correctly and make some changes if they aren't. This method isn't completely hands-off, but it's drastically less-intensive than finding motivated sellers, negotiating deals, rehabbing, finding tenants, and being a landlord.

There is literally an option for just about every level of workload in real estate. You can do as much or as little work as you'd like, depending on the strategy you choose. The key is finding a strategy that best fits you and your goals. Figuring out *what* strategy this is can take some time.

To get started in your exploration, you could:

- Read books on different real estate investment strategies.

- Attend seminars on various real estate investment strategies.

- Network with multiple people in the industry and find out more about what they do for their particular strategy.

- Visit real estate investing forums online and listen to what people are saying about different strategies (be sure to remember that anyone can say anything they want online, so be cautious about people who might sound like they know what they are talking about but really they might not).

While this book doesn't focus at all on the intricacies of each real estate investment strategy out there, know that you need to explore those to find the best approach for you. The most important thing to know is that options exist outside of swinging hammers. Once you start your research, it won't take long for you to find your way to the investment strategy that's right for you.

Myth: Statistics

Statistics can be insanely misleading. Data can be taken out of context, the source of the information or the parameters for the claims might be unreliable, and misinterpretation of the data might lead you to believe something that's not true. You have no way of knowing if you're making the correct interpretation using the information.

I hated most of my classes in high school, but one year I took an advanced-placement (AP) statistics course that has stuck with me ever since. My take-away from that class, whether my teacher intended for it or not, was how ridiculous and inaccurate so many statistics are. It's not always the numbers or the data itself but the interpretations people make about the numbers and the data. (This concept also helped me to realize that things in life aren't always what they seem, which turned out to be a profound realization.)

An example from the class I've always remembered was a statistic that said something like 95% of car accidents happen within a five mile radius of a person's house. The interpretation that readers took from that, and rightfully so, was that they needed to be extra cautious when driving closer to home because they were statistically more likely to be in an accident. Our challenge in the class was to look for any hidden information in the context of the statistic that might have caused the data or the interpretation to be inaccurate.

Can you see the problem with the statistic?

The reality was that, at the time and in the location in which that statistic was based, most people rarely drove much farther than five miles from their house. So the reason the statistic showed such a high probability of accidents within a five mile radius wasn't because it was more dangerous to drive closer to home, but it was because most driving was done within a five mile radius. Of course most of the accidents happen there because people weren't driving anywhere else.

Since then, I've questioned just about every statistic put in front of me. I don't question it because I want it to be wrong, but instead of believing the obvious conclusion, I make sure there isn't hidden information in the data or in the context that makes the results inaccurate or even dangerous.

For new real estate investors, statistics can be extremely misleading. For example, it makes my stomach turn every time I see a magazine or blog publish the newest list of 'good cities' for investing. Recent stories I've seen have titles like:

- The Top 10 Cities to Invest In
- The Most Profitable Cities for Real Estate Investors in 2023
- The Best Cities for Cash Flow in the U.S.
- The Top 10 Fastest Growing Cities in America

The one that notoriously drives me crazy is any title that sounds like the second one in the list above: *The Most Profitable Cities for Real Estate Investors in 2023*. When I read something like this, I cringe like I'm bracing for impact. That's because I know how many people will read it and, with the best of intentions, pursue investing in one of those cities, having absolutely no idea how dangerously misleading that list of cities likely is.

The biggest problem with that kind of list is that the author rarely specifies exactly what kind of investing they are referring to. '*The Most Profitable Cities for Real Estate Investors in 2023*'… for what exactly? Are they talking about buying rental properties, or are they talking about flipping properties? The fundamentals of rental property investing and flipping are completely different. While a city could be good for both, quite often that's not the case. What might be a great market for rental properties may not be advantageous for flippers, and what markets may be great for flippers might be extremely disadvantageous for rental property investors.

I'm not a confrontational person, but reading a list like *The Most Profitable Cities for Real Estate Investors in 2023* makes me want to go barreling into the author's office, point at the list, and then smack him over the head with it.

The reason I get worked up about this is that new investors, and even some experienced investors, don't know what they don't know. They don't know that this information may be extremely misleading. And in an industry like real estate investing, misleading information can cost someone a fortune.

Reading a data list or statistic should only prompt you to do some investigating. For instance, if a city is listed as being one of the best places to invest and you are investing in rental properties for cash flow, then check out whether or not that city actually has cash flow. There's a good chance it doesn't. The author was most likely thinking about what cities are the most stable and likely to appreciate, but stability and appreciation don't always have a bearing on cash flow.

Never just take data or statistics that someone puts out and run with them. If you're really interested in the information, find out more about the context in which it is intended and compare that to the fundamentals you know about your particular investment strategy and see if they fit together accurately.

Myth: Appreciation Will Always Happen

You can start by asking all the speculators how they felt about this one in 2008 when the entire market crashed and we entered into a recession…

The reality is that, over the long-term, appreciation will likely always happen. But in the short-term, appreciation is supposition; it's unpredictable. Even if appreciation does happen, that doesn't necessarily mean it will earn you a profit.

Some factors that affect the role appreciation will play on your bottom-line:

Where the property is located

Different cities have different historical appreciation trends. Cities like Los Angeles and San Francisco are known for appreciation and a lot of it. California, in general, is arguably the leading state for appreciation. Cities like Indianapolis and Kansas City and other Midwestern cities, however, are historically known to be stable markets. That means they tend not to crash as hard as other cities during recessions, but they also don't tend to appreciate much either. Then there are declining cities that not only don't appreciate, but they also lose value. Detroit has been a prime example of this over the years.

How much a city appreciates really depends on its basic market fundamentals and where the general real estate economy is at the time. For example, Atlanta and Dallas were two of the biggest appreciating cities coming out of the 2008 crash. But, historically, they aren't known for appreciation like Los Angeles or San Francisco, yet Los Angeles and San Francisco weren't the leaders in appreciation in those same years that Atlanta and Dallas were.

Market factors contributing to appreciation are often variable. And it's not just the nearest major city that affects appreciation— the neighborhood affects appreciation too. Is the neighborhood in a growing subset of the larger town? Is it in a safe area? Does it have desirable schools? Is it gentrifying? While some cities are thought of more suburb-by-suburb in terms of good and bad areas of town, other cities like Chicago can literally change from one street to the next. And how a neighborhood ranks in terms of these factors directly affects appreciation potential.

How much you pay for the property

Obviously the price you pay for the property will directly affect how much appreciation you can expect. Appreciation, in the context that you're going to look at it, is the difference between a property's value and what you paid for it.

How much you pay for a property can depend on several factors:

- the condition the property is in (ideally, the worse the condition, the lower the price)
- the state of the local real estate economy
- the stage of the market where you're buying
- how good of a deal you find

When you buy the property

How much you pay for a property often depends on when you buy the property. Real estate, in general, goes in cycles. Prices go up, prices go down, prices go up, prices go down. That's just what happens.

The general real estate economy is a timing issue. You've probably heard 'buy low, sell high'. This means buy when prices are low and sell when prices are high. It's not to say that if you buy high that you won't profit at all, but you lessen your chances, especially if appreciation is your only plan for profit. The best time to buy a property is during a crash. For investors, a crash is basically when properties go on sale. It doesn't mean you should just buy any property during a crash—you still need to consider the market and the property—but a crash or a recession is when you're going to find properties at their cheapest prices.

Using the 2008 crash as an example, 2007–2008 was a bad time to buy because prices were still high. But 2010–2011 was a great time to buy because prices had thoroughly tanked following the crash. That kind of timing can be scary for people. Low property values lessen investors' confidence that their investment will be safe, so a lot of people feel better doing it completely the opposite—buying at higher prices when their confidence is higher. But, as an investor who hopes to make money down the road, it's almost imperative you get your nerves on board and buy when prices are low.

When you sell the property

When you sell a property, if you sell it, is equally as important as when you buy. Using the same timeframe as above, 2008 was a great time to sell because prices were still high. But 2010–2011 was the worst time to sell because prices were at bottom following the crash.

The thing to realize about selling is that you never *have* to sell at any particular time. A common exception is when someone has bought a primary home for themselves and they either lose a job or experience some unforeseen circumstance so that they can no longer afford the house and are forced to sell. If the market is low at that time, they may lose a lot of money on the sale or have to foreclose or short sale. With investment properties, there's usually more room to maneuver on strategic market timing because the property is bringing in income, so you don't always have to sell low and lose money. If you're smart in how you buy the investment property, there are ways on the front-end to help mitigate crash circumstances. Nothing is ever guaranteed, but the first step in protecting against selling low is to realize that there are often options other than selling during a crash if you need them.

If you finance the property or not

This is a big one. And, surprisingly, it's one few people think about.

Let's say you buy your own home for $300,000 and you get a 30-year mortgage at a 5% interest rate with 20% down. At the end of the 30 years, you'll have paid roughly $252,000 in mortgage interest. That's in addition to the price of the house. You would need $252,000 in appreciation just to make up for the mortgage interest alone. That doesn't even include the appreciation necessary to cover all of the expenses during those 30 years (property taxes, insurance, improvements, repairs, etc.). If you pay cash, however, that's $252,000 less in appreciation you'd need to see to profit or break even. The mortgage interest on a loan can make or break whether you profit from appreciation.

With a good rental property, your tenants' payments will cover the mortgage interest as well as additional expenses. If you're flipping a house, the loan interest still comes into play, but because the deal happens on a shorter timeline, it's not such a big hit to the bottom line as it can be with a long-term hold property. Mortgage interest is less likely to impact appreciation profits on an investment property, but the point remains—don't forget about mortgage interest as an expense if you're financing a property, especially if you're banking on appreciation as your primary profit center.

At the end of the day, appreciation is speculative. It can be highly profitable, but it is far from guaranteed, and how you do it matters.

Myth: Real Estate is Riskier Than Other Investments

Real estate certainly can be risky. But the greatest risk comes when you don't know what you're doing. Whereas with stocks, for example, you can be totally clueless and just hand your money to someone and end up with a profit. If you're willing to learn what you need to in order to be half-competent at real estate investing, though, it'll offer two key opportunities that can give you an extra boost on your profitability; potentially a bigger boost than what stocks can offer:

Control

Unlike with stocks, you have control over your real estate investments. You can't control what the market is doing at any particular time, but you have options for how you adjust for it. You have options for how you run and manage a property; you have options to buy, sell, rent, finance, refinance, hire and fire contractors, make improvements, and evict tenants. That's a lot of room to maneuver.

When you put your money into stocks, the only thing you have control over is when you buy or sell the stock. You have no say with the company you've invested in. You have no say in their business decisions, course changes, problem prevention methods, or in finding ways to increase the value of the stock. You just have to sit and see what happens. Even day-traders, who move a lot faster with stocks and are very intricate with their transactions, are limited to only controlling when they buy and sell.

Having control over an investment isn't everyone's forte, but if it is your forte, having control over an investment can make a huge difference in profitability. Having the option to control profitability, if done correctly, decreases risk.

Multiple income streams

Stocks either increase in value or decrease in value, and that number reflects your profit or loss. There are no hidden streams of income or additional streams of income outside of that direct number. With real estate, there are.

Take rental properties, for example. There are actually five ways rental properties can make money:[1]

---

1   For details on each of these profit centers of a rental property go to www.aliboone.com/book-goodies.

1. monthly cash flow

2. appreciation

3. tax benefits

4. equity build via mortgage paydown

5. hedging against inflation

If at some point any of those income streams fail for some reason, you still have the potential of the other income streams to hopefully keep you going. Or if things are going really well, you have income (in some form) from five different directions on the same property. This is huge for risk mitigation. It's a unique advantage that stocks don't offer.

Myth: Any Property is a Good Investment

I once heard that roughly 80% of all properties make horrible investments. Once I got into the real estate investing world, I believed it.

For a property to be a good investment, it needs to make money.

A property may not make money if it:

- generates negative monthly cash flow
- is priced too high
- fails to resell at a desired value
- requires extensive repairs or rehab
- is located in a deteriorating neighborhood
- lacks rentability
- attracts low-quality tenants

Unfortunately, the list of ways a property could cost you money is pretty extensive. But when you know what the list is, you can shop smarter and learn to identify properties that do have solid income potential. And when you know what can cost you money as an investor, you can implement risk mitigations to help avoid problems down the road.

It's all about risk mitigation. Realizing most properties actually make horrible investments is the first step in mitigating your biggest risks.

Myth: The Best Investments Are the Ones with the Highest Returns

When you find good investment properties, the focus turns to the numbers. What return are you expecting on the property? Since the return on a real estate investment is the whole point in investing, it makes sense to focus on that bottom-line number.

While the numbers absolutely do matter, remember that numbers are *projected*. Whether or not those numbers actually pan out or not depends on a lot of factors. There is always a deeper story behind the digits, and you need to know what that story is.

For instance, there's no doubt that a bad tenant can be one of the most expensive things to happen to a rental property. You can find a property with the highest advertised cash flow possible, but if the property only attracts tenants that don't pay rent, consistently destroy the property, get evicted, and cause problems, you will never see that projected cash flow. And you'll probably have a lot of headaches.

The other possibility with the numbers is the idea of risk versus reward. Typically: the higher the projected returns, the higher the risk; the lower the projected return, the lower the risk. At least that's how it should go when everything is valued correctly. For example, do you buy a $40,000 property with a projected return of 15%, or do you buy a $100,000 property with a projected 9% return? If you just look at the numbers, the $40,000 property wins. But is there a catch? Yes, there is.

Typically, lower-priced properties, which are often of lower quality, can experience:

- more ongoing maintenance, if not substantially more work upfront
- a struggle to attract high-quality tenants
- limited exit strategy options[2]

Are the risks and headaches worth the extra amount of return? It may be worth it for some people and it may not be for others. Personally, I fall into the latter category. I'm fine with risk, but I'm adamantly opposed to headaches. I'll pay more and take the lower return all day long if it means I don't have to deal with as many problems. It's never a guarantee that the more expensive property with lower returns will offer fewer problems, but the odds are better than they are on a lower-priced high-return property.

The numbers are only projected and not proven, so it's possible that the higher projected return never happens. So, should you go for the property with the highest projected returns? Sometimes, sure, but not always because you may not actually ever see those returns, or if you do get them, you may hate your life.

Myth: You Have to Invest Locally to Where You Live

Back in the day when traveling was a bigger undertaking than it is today, you probably needed to invest locally to where you live. But in today's age of the internet, cell phones, cameras, and airplanes, there's really no reason you have to limit yourself to your own backyard for real estate investing.

---

2   Exit strategy refers to the end-game options for a property. Do you plan to sell it, and if so, do you plan to sell it to a primary homebuyer or an investor, do you plan to long-term hold it, do you plan to use future leveraging on it, etc. Exit strategy is key because it aids in the overall profit or loss on a property and it's your options for how to get rid of a property should you decide you don't want it anymore.

One of the strongest arguments people have for insisting you should only invest locally is that if something unexpected comes up with your property, you can get to it right away and handle it since you are nearby.

Let me put some perspective on this. I have a degree in Aerospace Engineering. I'm pretty smart. But if a tenant were to call me and say a toilet was overflowing or an oven was on fire or pipes had burst, I'd be about as useful as a rusted shovel on the top shelf of a barn with no ladder access if I showed up to the property and pretended to know what to do about the situation. Truly, I'm dumber than a gnat when it comes to common sense handy stuff. I'm the kind of person who will water a plant for months before realizing it's artificial (which has happened more than once). So, do you think I can do anything about pipes flooding a property? Even if I were near an overflowing toilet, what exactly would I do with it?

While I'd like to think I'd have an extra level of control over disasters on my properties if I were near them because I could get to them quickly, it's just not true. If I were handy, it might be another story. In that case, it would be nice to invest in something locally; I could save money by doing the work myself. But because I'm not handy, there's really no difference for me in calling a contractor or handyman from near the property or far away from the property, so it doesn't matter whether the property is local to me or not.

The key to non-local investing is the team you have helping you do it. When you invest outside of your local area, you have to implement teams to work on your investment properties. At that point, you switch roles: you go from being the manager of the technical details of a property and how it's run to being the manager of people. Personally, I like managing people better than I do toilets.

You don't necessarily decrease risk by investing locally like a lot of people want to claim. Yes, there is benefit to being able to see your investment property with your own eyes, but the risk isn't lower 100% of the time. Regardless of where the property is located, the risk level is going to be more directly tied to what kind of investment property you're investing in than it will be tied to where it's located. If you take on a massive flip project near where you live, that's going to be riskier than buying a rent-ready high-quality rental property non-local to where you live. It's all in what you're buying, how you're buying it, and how you're managing it.

If you understand the key components to any investment strategy, you can lower the risk and make it work. Investing non-locally to where you live is part of a strategy that you can master. The upside to being willing to invest non-locally is that when you're willing to invest in different areas, you can chase the highest profit potentials as they move around. When you aren't willing to invest non-locally, you'll be forced to work with the returns offered in your area.

A caveat to the argument for investing non-locally is that not everyone is cut out to trust other people to take care of an investment property on their behalf. When you invest outside of your local area, you are forced to rely on other people to either fully tend to your property on your behalf or to help you tend to it. I encourage everyone to exercise some honest self-awareness around your comfort levels with this. *If you will lose sleep by not having direct control over your investment property, ignore this whole idea and buy something local to you.* No investment is worth losing sleep over, no matter how profitable it might be. If you won't lose sleep entrusting your property to other people, however, you can absolutely maximize investment returns by allowing for the ability to invest where it makes the most sense, even if that's not in your backyard.

The Biggest Myth of All: Buying Your Own Home is a Good Investment

This one is my favorite because I was personally duped by this myth when I was younger. Not only was I duped by it, but I ran around screaming about how true it was. I even tried to convince people it was true.

My grandfather was an investor and entrepreneur. When he was still alive, he told all of the grandkids that if any of us wanted to pursue an investment, he would help us out financially. As soon as I got my first big-girl job as an engineer and was in a position to buy a house, I went running right to Grandpa's kitchen table and told him I was ready to buy a house, reminding him about his offer to help with an investment.

In a really gruff voice, he said, "That's not an investment."

I said, "Of course, it is, Grandpa. It's the first investment anyone makes. It's an investment and it's smart."

He gruffly repeated, "That's not an investment."

He didn't say another word, and he didn't forfeit a penny toward my 'investment' journey.

When I told my dad about this encounter, his response was, "Well, it's not an investment."

I thought Dad and Grandpa had just been hit in the head by aliens. Of course buying my first house was an investment! I was sure of it. I had heard that message my entire life. How could the whole world be wrong?

It wasn't until years later, long after I bought that first house, that I read *Rich Dad Poor Dad* and, consequently, got into real estate and suddenly realized why Dad and Grandpa had said buying my own home wasn't an investment. Apparently I needed to hear it from a total stranger, Robert Kiyosaki, to believe it before I believed it from my own family.

The problem with the logic that a primary house is an investment comes down to the true expense of maintaining a property over the period of time you own it. Several articles and a lot of research have come out now that breaks down the true expenses of owning a house. I'm not going to get into the math here, but you can search 'the true expense of owning a house' in any search engine and see the numbers.

Most people think they will get back all the money they put into their house once they sell. That may be true for the mortgage principle, but there are a lot of other expenses that come with owning a house. The expenses on your primary home will include property taxes, insurance, maintenance, repairs, utilities, improvements, and homeowner's association (HOA) fees or condo fees if applicable... just to name a few. Those are unavoidable expenses on any property. Tallying up those expenses throughout the time you own the home may blow your socks off. And, as I clarified earlier, if you own a property as your primary home, it's not generating income to offset those expenses.

Of those expenses, though, enter the real monster stage left—the mortgage interest. I already mentioned this issue, but I'm going to bring it up again and go into deeper detail.

If you pay for your house in cash and don't get a mortgage, this conversation drastically changes. But I'll assume you're buying with a mortgage. Within the mortgage payment, part of each payment goes toward the principal of the loan—the actual cost of the house—and part of each payment goes toward the interest on the loan. The principal isn't the concerning factor because any money paid toward that will be recuperated in the equity on the home. The concerning factor is the interest.

The mortgage payment is amortized over 30 years (or whatever term applies to your loan) and the interest is always paid off first. So each month the interest on the remaining principal balance is calculated and that amount is paid toward the interest. Whatever's left goes toward the principal. As time goes on, the interest portion of your payment gets smaller while the principal portion of your payment gets larger. If you only own a house for a few years as opposed to the full length of the loan term, most of the money you spend on the mortgage payment will have gone toward paying down the interest, not paying down much of the principal, which means little, if any, equity recoup for you.

Let's say, though, that you keep the house for the full 30 years of the term, so you have recouped all of your equity. How much interest will you have paid over those 30 years? Let's look at a basic example. You buy a $200,000 house with 20% down and a 5% interest rate on a 30-year mortgage. After the loan is paid off, you'll have spent $149,209.25 in interest. That's basically $150,000. That's almost the initial cost of the house. But then, what if you buy the house with a Federal Housing Administration (FHA) loan that lets you buy with only 5% down? Now you'll have spent $177,185.99 in interest, which isn't drastically different. But then you'll also have to pay Private Mortgage Insurance (PMI) because you didn't put 20% down, which can range from 0.5%–1% of the total price of the house per year. So then you're looking at another $1,000-2,000 per year in extra expenses on top of the additional interest. Either way, what matters is how much you spend on interest and PMI. Then add that to the list of other expenses mentioned—property tax, insurance, etc.—and come up with your total expenses over the course of owning the house. What's that number?

Since this is a primary home and not an investment property, meaning you aren't collecting income on it, your only hope of profit is with appreciation. How much does the property need to appreciate for you to actually profit? Well, what was that expense number? For that $200,000 property, the value of that property would basically have to double just to compensate for the mortgage interest expense alone. That's not even including what you spent on property taxes, insurance, closing costs, agent fees, maintenance, repairs, improvements, and any other expenses over the years you own the property. By the time all of that is said and done, it's likely your property will have had to triple or quadruple in value, at a minimum, to let you see a profit.

Can you see the problem with buying your own home as an investment strategy? The point of an investment is to make a financial gain. Where does the financial gain come from on your own home? Certainly, there are situations where it can work. You can find a distressed property and rehab it while you live in it so you force the appreciation. Or you can buy during a major market crash so you're buying at a massive discount, and the market will bring the value up for you over time. But even with both of those scenarios, the numbers still need to work for it to be profitable.

People opposed to this view argue that at least the money you put toward a mortgage, as compared to what you pay in rent, is money you recoup later. This may be true, and it may not. It's going to depend on your location and how rental rates compare to property prices. In the location of that $200,000 house you were thinking of buying (until I killed your dreams...), figure out what you would likely pay in rent in that area. Tally up that total over the 30 years, or however long you own the property, see what that total expense would be, and compare that to the total expense of having bought the house. The numbers may not be what you expect.

Well, what's the alternative? My personal favorite, which is the same alternative that Robert Kiyosaki suggests, is to buy investment properties rather than my own property. Remember all of those expenses I listed for a primary home? On an investment property, all of those expenses can either be written-off on your taxes or covered by your tenants through their rent payment. Then any cash flow or appreciation gain you see, as well as equity paydown, is free money to you. Now THAT is an investment.

Not to be all emo about it, but I think it's fair to say in this day and age that the 'American Dream' of owning your own home as a good investment is dead. Or at least it should be.

part two

Perspectives That Will
Blow Your Mind[set]

chapter three

The Power of Passive Income

Here's where all of this starts to get juicy.

It's said that passive income is income you don't have to work for. Sometimes you'll hear it referenced as money you can make in your sleep. While this is technically true, there's a misconception sometimes about passive income. Some people take this to mean they'll never have to do any work for said income, which is rarely true. It can take quite a bit of work up front to generate passive income, like seeking knowledge and educating yourself to be able to secure passive income. And once you're getting passive income, there's often some maintenance work you need to do to keep the passive income flowing.

For example, you own a rental property and employ a property manager to handle the landlording duties for you. The income from that rental property will continue to come in without the need for you to work directly with tenants or toilets all the time. However, if you let years go by and you never check in on the property manager or only occasionally upgrade the property, the income will likely stop at some point. So you do end up making money in your sleep since you aren't actively required for the income to come in, but it doesn't mean you never have to put some effort toward the investment.

But apart from setting up and maintaining the income stream, passive income allows you to collect income while you sleep.

That's the key—the money comes in even when you aren't working. This leads to a level of freedom unbeknownst to most.

If someone were to live fully off passive income, meaning they never had to be present in any particular place in order to receive that income, what would their life look like? Well, it could look like whatever they want it to. Think about it. How much time and commitment do you have tied into your 9-to-5 job? It's not just the 40+ hours you work that holds you down. Add commute time to those daily hours. Also, add preparation and decompression time—the time you spend getting ready for work and the time you spend recovering from work when you get home. Then consider the fact that where you live is completely dependent on where you work. Unless you work from home, you can't live just anywhere; you must live in some proximity to your job. So think, 10–14 hours per day dedicated to your job in some fashion, roughly, and you're restricted to living in a particular place.

Unless you love your job and like the place you live, can you see how much you're potentially missing out on in life? You have time for little else during the week outside of your work, and you may not be able to experience a lot of things you enjoy because you're tied to a certain location by your job.

Take away the job, and what does that look like? Pretend you really did have enough passive income to support your lifestyle so you didn't have to work at all. What would your day look like then, as opposed to the 10–14 hours related to work and the fact that you live far away from things you love to do?

One word: retirement.

Think of what people do when they're retired. They don't have to be up at a certain time, they can relax all day if they want to, they can travel anytime they want to, they can go visit family and friends anytime they want to, and they attempt to do all the things they've always wanted to do but never had a chance to while they were working.

This is exactly what you would be able to do if all of your income was passive. When you have the freedom to design your days exactly how you want them to be because you don't have to be at a job, you're experiencing lifestyle design.

Lifestyle design means designing your life to be exactly what you want it to be, whatever that may be. If you were able to clear your entire schedule for next week and design that week to be whatever you wanted it to be, what kinds of things would you include in it? Here are some things, some obvious and some less obvious, that you can include in your personal lifestyle design:

- living wherever you want
- sleeping in as late as you want
- going to bed as late as you want
- watching TV anytime you want
- volunteering
- trying new hobbies
- wearing whatever clothes or outfits you want
- learning new things (e.g., going back to school for a totally irrelevant degree)
- traveling anywhere you want for however long you want
- hanging out with friends and family anytime you want
- going to places during the week that are miserably crowded on the weekends (brunch spots, ski slopes, parks, bars, Disneyland…)
- and the list goes on

The world is at your fingertips when you're no longer tied to a 9-to-5 job. In all fairness, though, not everyone has the goal of achieving complete financial freedom or will ever obtain it. For some, passive income is helpful as just extra income. Extra income can help with financial security, retirement funds, and general sanity. Passive income options allow for more people to have financial flexibility and security without taking on a second job or adding more tasks to their already busy schedule. Someone who has a 40-hour work week and a spouse and kids probably doesn't have time to take on a second job if they want extra income. They could, however, invest in passive income investments and let their money work for them while they tend to their other priorities.

There are whole books written on the subject of passive income. Some books talk about why passive income is so important. There are other books about various business principles for getting passive income. And some books, like *The 4-Hour Workweek* by Tim Ferriss, even go into detail about the awesomeness that lifestyle design allows for thanks to having passive income.

There are many ways to create passive income. In terms of generating passive income through real estate investing, the key is understanding the concept of investing versus working. When you understand the difference between investing and working, you'll begin to see the passive income options more clearly. Don't worry, there's a whole chapter about it coming up.

Additionally, the IRS taxes active and passive income differently. Active income, such as income you receive from wholesaling or flipping (because those are considered active strategies, just like your job is considered active), is much less tax-advantaged than passive income. Passive income tax breaks are so great that you often end up paying nothing in income tax because the extensive write-offs make up for what you would otherwise pay in taxes. This may not seem like a huge thing, but when you calculate a third of your income and realize you don't have to pay that to the government, you might suddenly see the tax advantage of passive investments. At the time I write this, residential rental properties—meaning four units or less—are the most tax-advantaged asset class available for investors. Rental properties are considered passive investments, so maximum tax benefits are available on those.

No one *has* to have passive income to succeed. Plenty of people succeed all the time with purely active income. The key though is to know your goals and be able to tailor your investments to fit those goals, which often brings into play the concept of passive income.

chapter four

The Three True Currencies

We trade money for things we want. I want an apple, I give someone money in exchange for it. I want a house, I give someone money in exchange for one. If someone wants something of mine, they can give me money in exchange for it.

As the name implies, currency means 'in circulation'. In the cases mentioned above, money is in circulation as a medium of exchange. If currency just means 'in circulation' though, is money the only thing that can be considered a currency?

Most people only think about money when they think of a currency. But when I look at everything I do in life, I very clearly see that money isn't the only form of currency I use on a daily basis. In fact, it's not even the most important currency I use. On any given day, I'm likely giving or receiving any one of these three currencies, or some combination thereof:

1. money
2. time
3. sanity

In the same way I give money in exchange for something, I can just as easily give my time in exchange for something. I can also be forced to give up some of my sanity in exchange for something.

Let's say I want custom shelves built for my living room. I have two options for getting these shelves built:

1. Hire someone to build them for me.

2. Build them myself.

Most people focus only on one currency when it comes to this kind of situation, and that's money. The common argument against hiring someone to do anything is usually the money that can be saved by not hiring the person. Following this argument, I decide I should save the money I would pay someone else and just build the shelves myself.

In thinking of building shelves, I have a couple of considerations in play. First, I have no idea how to build shelves. In addition to that, I'm not naturally skilled at that kind of work. As I've mentioned earlier, I'm not that crafty so figuring out how to build them probably wouldn't come very easily or naturally to me. The second consideration is that I don't particularly like to stress over things I'm not good at and don't enjoy. And a third consideration is that since books are heavy, if I don't build the shelves just right I risk the entire shelf collapsing and tearing out a chunk of the wall when I fill it with books.

It's clear then that if I build the shelves myself, I'm going to pay for the shelves with two things: my *time* and my *sanity*. The time part would be a reality for anyone building something on their own, and the sanity part would be specific to me or anyone else who has absolutely no interest or natural skill in that kind of work. Therefore, while I just saved myself the money I would've paid someone else to build the shelves, I just paid for the shelves with the two lesser-known currencies: time and sanity.

When I was about 13, I remember thinking I wanted to make a gazillion dollars when I grew up. It felt like a fun personal challenge to figure out how to make that happen. Throughout college, I held onto that goal of wanting to make a lot of money, and the idea played a significant role in my initial career choices.

It wasn't until I became an entrepreneur though that I started to change my priorities.

Once I got a taste of what I described earlier as 'lifestyle design' and entrepreneurship, my time and sanity suddenly became much bigger players in my life, taking a huge priority over money. I realized that I would much rather not make a gazillion dollars if it meant not donating all of my time or sanity to what I was doing. While I was initially pumped at the idea of making a gazillion dollars and certainly wouldn't complain if that happens in the future, I realized that my time (for sleeping in and snowboarding and lying on the beach) and my sanity (for all things happiness) are two things I'm not willing to give up in order to get that money.

That means: my time and my sanity are worth more to me than money is. Therefore, it may be cheaper for me to pay more for something monetarily than if I try to save the money and do it myself. Do you see why?

If I rank each currency—money, time, and sanity—in order of which is most important to me, my list would look like:

1. sanity
2. time
3. money

Meaning, sanity is my most valued commodity. Time is my second most valued, and both of those are more important to me than money. Your list may look different, but that's how I rank the currencies for myself.

So when I ask myself what's the cheapest way for me to get something or have something done, I'm forcing myself to assign value to each form of currency so I can more accurately weigh out my cheapest option. While money apparently is my cheapest option, there may be times where I don't mind spending the time on a project and it won't necessarily cost me any of my sanity. In those cases, maybe I do spend some of my time to save some money.

In some cases, it might be perfectly fine for me to pay less for something that I put more work into in the cases where doing so doesn't cost me any sanity. The important part is not so much which currency I save on, but it's in being clear on exactly what I'm spending on something. Most people never consider that they're spending time or sanity on something.

It's rare that you can buy something or have something done that doesn't cost you at least one of the currencies. The question is: which currency is more expensive for you? The answer to this will be different for everyone, and it will be different for various projects or purchases. Flipping a house would not only cost me massive amounts of time and sanity, both of which are invaluable to me. So it's better for me to use money to pay more for the rent-ready rental property, in order to save my time and sanity. For other people, flipping a house may not only come easily to them, but it might even bring them joy. In that case, it makes sense to save on the money rather than the time and sanity.

How do you rank the three currencies for yourself? Make #1 the currency you consider to be the most valuable to you, which means it's your most expensive currency. #3 should be the currency you consider to be the least valuable to you of all of them, which means it's your cheapest currency. You can list them here:

#1 _____

#2 _____

#3 _____

Once you're clear on which currencies are the most valuable to you, be sure to always keep those in mind as you make decisions both in real estate investing and in life. You'll be surprised at how much more enjoyable things get when they truly align with your priorities.

chapter five

Using Other People's Money

There's always the option of using money as a currency, but rather than using your own money, you can use someone else's. You'll see this sometimes referred to as "leveraging" or using OPM: other people's money.

OPM can come from several different sources, including but not limited to:

- banks
- credit unions
- private lenders
- credit cards
- investment partners
- seller-financing
- family & friends

Aside from the obvious situation of not having enough of your own money to invest with, so you have to use someone else's money, there's also the scenario of having enough of your own money to invest but choosing to use someone else's money anyway. Why would you consider doing that if you can just use your own money? Two reasons:

1. At some point, you'll run out of your own money which will cause you to have to stop investing.

2. The returns when you leverage other people's money have an infinitely higher return potential.

Running out of money eventually is just a fact. You only have a finite pool of resources, and once that pool is depleted, that's the end of it. The only way to expand your resources past what you have is to use other people's money, whether solely or in addition to your own money.

But a higher return potential? That one may need some explanation. How could I end up with higher returns by using someone else's money, especially if I'm likely paying interest on the borrowed funds?

Doing the Math

You buy a $100,000 rental property in cash. You collect $1000/month in rent and $700/month after expenses. Calculating the cash-on-cash return on that gives you an 8.4% return on your money.[3]

Now you buy a $100,000 rental property with a mortgage instead of paying by cash. The property has the same income and expense numbers as before, but now you also have to subtract the $430 mortgage payment[4] each month. Now you're only getting $270/month in cash flow after expenses. But when you compare that $270/month to having only put $20,000 down instead of $100,000 (20% down payment versus paying the full purchase price in cash), your cash-on-cash return now jumps to 16.2%.

Having leveraged this particular $100,000 rental property gives you a 16.2% return on your money whereas buying it outright gives you only an 8.4% return on your money. You've just doubled the returns. And that's just the cash flow returns.

Now think, because you only spent $20,000 on the $100,000 property having used a mortgage, and assuming you have $100,000 to

---

3   Cash-on-Cash Return = [Annual Net Income (including the mortgage payment)]/
     [Cash Invested]*100
4   Calculated with a 5% interest rate with a 20% down payment

invest (and that's why you thought about possibly paying cash), you could then buy five properties instead of having only been able to buy the one for $100,000.

Using the same numbers as above, at $270/month in cash flow, if you have five properties, you're now bringing in $1,350/month. So for the same $100,000 investment ($100,000 cash put into one property or $100,000 split between five properties at 20% down each), you're coming out with a higher cash flow every month.

But wait, there's more.

In addition to cash flow, a rental property can see income from appreciation, tax benefits, equity build via mortgage paydown, and indirect income when the property serves as a hedge against inflation.

Looking just at appreciation, say your $100,000 property appreciates to $150,000. You've now gained $50,000 in equity, which is essentially free money. If you bought just the one property, you'd gain just that $50,000. But what if you bought five of those properties and they all appreciated by $50,000? You'd have gained $250,000 in free money ($50,000 gain x five properties) instead of just $50,000.

There's a big difference between $250,000 and $50,000, and the bank isn't keeping that money—that money is yours. Higher cash flow per month and 5x the appreciation. Then add in 5x the tax benefits, 5x the equity build via mortgage paydown, and all of those properties are hedging against inflation. Then you've also introduced some risk mitigation against vacancy as well because if one property goes vacant, you have the income from the other four to keep you afloat during that period of no income from the one property.

The numbers mentioned are arbitrary and not inclusive of all of the costs of buying a property, but they demonstrate even still the financial power of leveraging. You're looking at roughly five times the financial power of your investment, all because you were willing to leverage your money.

Creative Financing Options

There are other ways to leverage money outside of traditional mortgages. In fact, figuring out creative ways to leverage money in real estate investing is one of the primary things that sets successful empire-builders apart from other investors. A lot of people don't start out with a lot of capital to invest with, and maybe they don't qualify for a mortgage or loan. What do those people do? Well, that's where the 'creative' part comes in. If you can figure out ways to intelligently finance deals, you're likely going to be on a clear path to success.

I can give you an example of something I did in the early years with my rental properties. After the Nicaragua bust, I was short on cash. But some deals popped up that I really wanted in on. At the time, I had about $10,000 I could invest. This was around 2011 when recession prices were still in full swing, so I could easily buy a great rental property with $10,000 and a mortgage. I knew I could do this for one property, but once that $10,000 was gone, what would I use to buy more?

Hello, creative financing!

I brought in an investment partner for a number of properties at this time.[5] This investment partner had multiple sets of $10,000 available. But what could I offer him in exchange for using his

---

5   Choosing an investment partner is not something you should take lightly. Partnering can be dangerous if you don't take the proper precautions. Legal partnership agreements should always be in place to protect you and your assets. Consult a real estate attorney before entering into any partnership agreement.

money? We agreed to use his cash and my credit to buy the deals. He covered the down payments, and I took the mortgages in my name and did all the work. So he put up the money, and I put up the risk. We agreed this constituted a 50/50 split in contribution. So once we bought the properties, we split everything down the middle 50/50—profit or loss. Every month when we collected cash flow, he got half and me the other half. If major expenses came up, we split them down the middle. If we decided to sell, we split the profit or loss down the middle. For him, this setup was nice because he was able to invest money with no hit to his credit or mortgage ability (you can only get so many mortgages in your name). And I ended up with, essentially, infinite returns because I had no money into the properties.

That's only one of the many options for creative solutions to financing. Other financing options may include loans outside of traditional mortgages. Maybe you roll equity from one property into another property. There's no end to the possibilities for how to finance investments. The key is to make sure you know the particulars of each option and you choose an option that makes sense for your situation.

Figuring out creative financing solutions is arguably the crux of building an empire. You can learn a lot from people who have already done it themselves, but they can only take you so far. In the end, you really have to figure a lot of it out on your own. Figuring out creative financing solutions is almost like a rite of passage for successful investors—few empire-owners find success without creative financing.

The Risk

There are a million arguments out there about how leveraging is extremely risky. If done irresponsibly, leveraging other people's money can absolutely be risky.

For example, you buy a rental property with an adjustable rate loan. In the beginning, the property cash flows well and is profitable. But all of a sudden, the rate adjustment happens and for whatever reason the interest rate skyrockets. Now you're in a negative cash flow situation, which could be one of many compounding problems.

Another example is if you use a hard money loan on a flip. You borrow the money, which usually comes with a high interest rate because it's a short-term loan, and all of a sudden the flip project takes a bad turn—like the rehab cost becomes prohibitive so you can't finish the project, and now you can't sell the property for what you planned—and now the loan payoff is due.

However, if you know what you're doing and you're smart on how you structure the leveraging, you can drastically minimize leveraging risks.

In the case of that rental property, it's critical to get a fixed-rate loan instead of an adjustable-rate loan. If you combine a fixed-rate loan with the property being in a solid growth area with the ability to attract high-quality tenants, your leveraging risks decrease dramatically.

In the case of flipping a property with hard money, while the loan structure doesn't necessarily change, it's critical that you understand exactly what you're doing as a flipper in order to minimize risk. The concept of flipping is easy—buy a distressed property, rehab it, sell it for more than you paid for it—but flipping can come with a lot of challenges that new investors aren't aware of. Those unexpected challenges can put the investor at major risk for not being able to pay back that loan. Another way to decrease risk in this scenario is to establish a contingency plan for the loan payback ahead of time, should the flip not go as planned.

There's no contesting that using other people's money in real estate investing is not only incredibly financially advantageous, but it's also required in a lot of cases if you want to continue to build your portfolio. Ultimately though, financial success is a variable measure, as is any kind of success. One person's perception of success may be wildly different from someone else's perception of success. There are some people who are pleasantly content keeping their portfolios small. There are also some people who may feel so uncomfortable with leveraging—using other people's money—that no level of financial success is worth the weight they might feel worrying about it. In both of those cases, there's no requirement to go wild with financial creativity. But if you do choose to take advantage of the opportunity to leverage other people's money in your investing, you really do open up the potential for infinite expansion.

part three

Put Your Snorkel On
Before You Dive In

chapter six

Don't Shave Years off Your Life

If you take just one thing away from reading this book, let it be this: *no investment is worth losing your sanity.* You can find the most profitable real estate investment deal out there, the deal of the century, but if pursuing that deal will cause you to lose sleep at night at any point, it's not worth it. I don't think life is about numbers. For me, life is about happiness, and there is really no dollar amount that can be assigned to happiness. This also pertains to life beyond real estate. There are way too many options available in life for you to sacrifice any amount of your sanity for something.

As mentioned earlier, a major advantage to real estate investing is that there are so many options for how you can do it that you can likely find a strategy that both puts money in your pocket *and* lets you sleep at night. Because there are so many options, you can choose not only what keeps you sane but also what keeps you happy. That's not to say there will never be stress involved in whichever real estate investing route you choose, but there needs to be an underlying satisfaction and ease that keeps you moving through those stresses because otherwise it will be very easy and tempting to give up.

When choosing an investment strategy, my approach is to play to my strengths. Have you ever heard of 'strengthening your strengths' rather than strengthening your weaknesses? What happens if we're willing to improve on our strengths rather than trying to improve on our weaknesses?

Picture a bar graph that compares your skills or characteristics, showing which ones you're strong in and which ones you're weak in.

I've created one for myself:

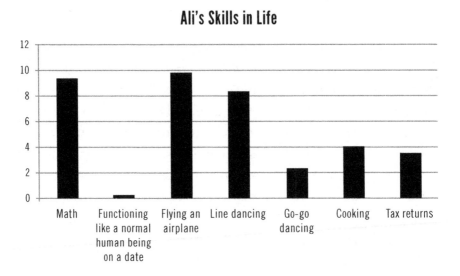

The higher the bar, the stronger I am in that skill. The lower the bar, the weaker I am.

If I were to follow the old myth that says I should try to strengthen my weaknesses, I would work on the low bars. To demonstrate my point, I'm going to ignore the 'functioning like a normal human being on a date' because I'm not even sure how to work on that one. So let's say then that I'm going to work on go-go dancing, cooking, and learning how to do my tax returns because I'd like to be stronger in those areas. To (attempt to) strengthen those weaknesses, I sign up for cooking classes, dance classes, and tax courses. Let's look at the progress I make in each of those areas in graph form:

Ali's Skills in Life—
Strengthening the Weaknesses

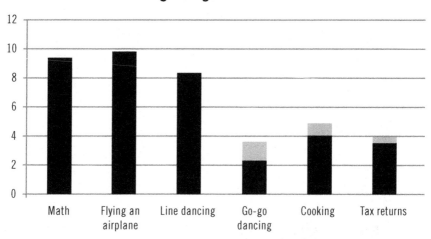

You can see on the graph how much I was able to improve in those skills by trying to strengthen them. Go-go dancing improved the most because I actually wanted to learn to go-go dance.[6] Cooking improved a little, but I didn't really like it so it only went so far. And tax returns... well, I fell asleep trying.

In two of the three skills, I didn't even like what I was trying to do. Ever notice how it's not very common to enjoy things you're terrible at? I could keep trying to learn go-go dancing, and even enjoy trying to learn it, but the fact will never change that go-go dancing is not one of my natural strengths. I'm not even good at walking in high heels much less dancing in them.

Now that you've seen the data following me trying to work on my weaknesses, let's see how I did when I worked to try to improve my natural strengths of math, flying an airplane, and line dancing instead:

---

6   Side note: I actually did try to become a go-go dancer, so I can speak to the accuracy of the poor results of that one.

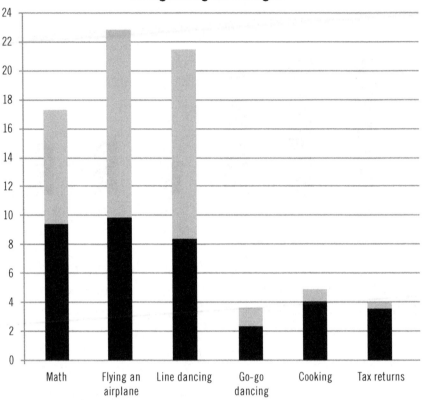

Ali's Skills in Life—
Strengthening the Strengths

Look how much more I was able to strengthen my strengths compared to my how much I was able to strengthen my weaknesses. These are all hypothetical scenarios, but they're built on the premise that we all excel at things we're naturally good at and that we enjoy doing. And don't we tend to enjoy things more when we're excelling at them? Notice that cycle—the more we excel at something, the more we enjoy it, and the more we enjoy it, the more we excel at it. And most often, both of these things—joy and the ability to excel—are related to our natural skill sets.

I didn't just make up how all this works—it's actual science. Clifton-Strengths[7] is a great resource if you want to read more about this.

---

7 Get a link to check out CliftonStrengths at www.aliboone.com/book-goodies

This is what I mean by going with your natural grain. It's so common that people tell us we need to strengthen our weaknesses, but why should we? If we can't be great at everything in life, why not focus on the things we're naturally inclined toward and that we enjoy more?

It's good to step out of your comfort zone sometimes and try to improve in areas less familiar to you. I 100% advocate you doing that, but I don't necessarily advocate you doing that in an attempt to make yourself into someone you aren't. Instead, do it on the side or when you have enough spare time (or money) to do it for fun.

As a real estate investor, there's no question that my natural grain is with rental properties. The knack for handling rental properties has always come naturally to me; I understand the process and I've always been effortlessly good at dealing with them. Would I have chosen rental properties as my preferred investment choice? No, I would've picked flipping. Not only could I make a lot of money in a short amount of time flipping houses, but it seems like flipping would be fun. However, if you saw me try to negotiate a deal or manage a contractor, you'd know flipping isn't part of my natural grain. I currently own the world's most expensive bookshelves at my house, not because they're fancy shelves, but because I can be so gullible with contractors. So while flipping seems like the most advantageous choice I could make for a real estate investment strategy on the surface, the reality of it is that it's not at all the smartest choice for me.

With rental properties, though, I can slide up that strengths bar with no problem whatsoever. If I wanted to learn to flip, I could, but while the concept of flipping sounds exciting, all the skills necessary for flipping sound miserable to me. And because the skills are so unnatural to me, I could probably only get so good at it. That's not to say I should never flip a property, as I do think it could be a fun side project and I could learn a lot, but for me it needs to be exactly that—a fun side project rather than one I'm relying on for income. When I'm relying on something for income, I need an option that I can move more quickly with and without taking on too much risk by doing things I'm not good at.

Now that my inner bar graph nerd has shown its face, I hope you understand what I'm saying about focusing on what comes most naturally to you. There are plenty of reasons to stay focused on those things.

If you don't already have an idea of what comes naturally to you, and most of us don't, it's easy to start keeping an eye out for those things. Start by trying different options within real estate investing. Take courses, read books, and attend seminars. You don't have to break the bank here, but finding what comes more effortlessly to you starts with educating yourself about what options are out there. During this time, you'll find that you begin to gravitate toward certain opportunities over others.

There are two things to be on the lookout for as you start exploring:

1. **What you enjoy the most.** We're often taught to believe that hard work is what leads to success. That may be true, but no one ever said you can't enjoy it along the way. I find that the more naturally inclined I am at something, the more I enjoy it. So, why not hack that equation a little and let what you enjoy show you what you're naturally good at?

2. **What presents itself to you the most.** As you explore real estate and gather experience, you might notice certain types of opportunities come to you more than others. Which real estate options seem to come to you over and over again? This is something to pay attention to.

I was able to figure out what comes naturally for me in real estate investing because of the second point I mentioned. It really felt like I didn't choose rental properties—they chose me. I had been researching and studying everything under the sun *except* for rental properties, and yet they showed up. They came to me so naturally and easily that I was able to move faster on them than I ever expected, and I even started a business with them.

Do I enjoy rental properties? Yes and no. They are what they are. I do like shopping for new ones to buy and analyzing the numbers. Once I've purchased them, I have a property manager who does the work on them—finding and screening tenants, taking repair calls, managing contractors, maintaining contracts and legal work, and handling emergencies—so I'm mostly hands-off and not overly involved with them. I admit though that I don't particularly like dealing with tenant problems, even if they are being managed by the property manager. I do like the passive income I get from the properties each month though, and tax time has even been more enjoyable since I bought rental properties because of the extra returns I get for the properties. For me though, they are really more of a vehicle for what it is I want—passive income— than something I'm overly passionate about. But still, they come very naturally to me.

I mentioned earlier that I had at least some reason to believe that I wasn't very good at managing contractors. In the case of the bookshelves, I was unassumingly gullible with a contractor who took advantage of me. I've had plenty of experiences with good contractors also, but I was repeatedly noticing how little I liked dealing with them even still. This was confirmed a few years into owning one of my rental properties when a tenant destroyed the whole interior of the property with smoke damage, and I had to get the property fully rehabbed. Just managing the rehab project—not even getting my hands dirty—was exhausting. Between getting completely taken by the first contractor I had working on the property and then having to spend two weeks overseeing the next contractor, I hated every minute of it. Making trips to Home Depot multiple time a day, constantly fighting traffic, watching the expense tallies ring up, having to coordinate different people to help finish the property, and constantly finding things that weren't done correctly was not my cup of tea.

Rehabs? No thank you. If ramming myself face-first into a wall wouldn't have created more work for the contractor, I would've done it on the daily trying to manage that rehab. I got a great property out of it, and I was able to rent it for way more than I could have pre-rehab, but I never want to manage a rehab again.

The bottom line is this: swimming upstream with real estate investing, or with anything in life, just causes frustration. I firmly believe you can't succeed by going against your natural grain in the same way that you can when you do something that comes naturally to you. It may take you some time to figure out what you enjoy and what you're good at, but make that part of the learning process.

Following what comes most naturally to you will lead to your greatest success. That means achieving financial success *and* gaining that success with ease and enjoyment. Don't be the fish that constantly tries to swim upstream. Let your own flow carry you and you'll find that investing will just be easier.

chapter seven

Investing vs. Working

As people start getting into real estate investing, one of the biggest unknowns to new investors is the true level of work that will be required for any given investment strategy.

Let's break down two critical terms here: *investing* and *working*.

> Investing: *money* is the means to the profit
> Working: *effort* is the means to the profit

With stocks, you hand your money over, you do nothing other than maybe occasionally glance at the stock prices, and then at some point, you pull the money out. The money you earn on your stock investment is pure investment. You do no work, so all of the profits come from the investment itself. Investing in real estate notes would be similar to this. You invest in the note and do no work, so any profit you make on that investment is straight from the investment itself.

Most people go into real estate investing intending to achieve the same thing—an investment. They're looking for a return on their money. They want to put some amount of money into an investment project or opportunity, and they want to get a return on that money in the form of more money. That's exactly how an investment works, and it makes sense that it's what people hope to achieve by getting into real estate as an investment strategy.

Things can go a little wonky, though, when people don't realize that some real estate investment strategies require an absurd amount of work. Work isn't a bad thing, but it's different from investing.

In the case of some real estate investing strategies, your investment return is directly based on how much work you put in. If you have to put work into an investment, your profits will be a mixture of 1) investment and 2) compensation for your time and effort (work).

Use flipping a property as an example. You buy a distressed property and fund the rehab. That's your financial investment. But then you rehab the house yourself. You spend time fixing and improving things and managing contractors. Let's say you spend 200 hours working on rehabbing this property over four months. If you're being honest about the profit you make on the flip, you would consider part of that profit as compensation for those 200 hours you spent on the project and the remainder would be the actual return on investment, rather than it all being profit from the investment.

The reason it's imperative to distinguish what's prompting your financial gain is a) you want to make sure you're earning your goal amount on your investment and b) you need to know ahead of time what kind of time and work requirement this particular investment is going to require so you know whether you can feasibly do it, or if you even want to do it.

Every investment strategy is going to require a different amount of *work*. To give you an idea, here are some of the most popular real estate investment strategies:

- *wholesaling:* all work, no investment
- *flipping:* half work, half investment[8]

---

8   There are ways to structure the active strategies so that it's an outsourced business which would decrease your workload. But for the intent of this point, assume you are doing the work.

- *landlording rental properties:* half work, half investment
- *using property managers on rental properties:* minimal work, mostly investment
- *notes and REITS:* no work, all investment

Again, why does this matter? Because you have to weigh the implications of working for your investments against your:

√ skill level

√ interest level

√ availability

√ risk tolerances

Personally, I have plenty of availability and risk tolerance to be able to get crazy with my investments. My skill level is so-so—I'm not good at doing technical pieces of work myself, but I'm good at project management, so I could manage contractors if I needed to. Where I fall short, though, is with my interest level. To say I have absolutely no interest in working on my investments would be an understatement. I get frustrated, I get no joy out of managing contractors, I don't like waking up early to meet contractors, I prefer to work as little as possible for my money, and I hate being tied down or required to be anywhere at any particular time.

When I look at this level of self-awareness, I can begin to better gauge what investment strategies might be a good fit for me. This assessment will be different for everyone, and it's up to you to be honest with yourself. Otherwise, you may quickly end up hating your investments.

Wholesaling Is NOT Investing

One of the most popular real estate investing strategies pitched to newbie investors is wholesaling. Wholesaling is where you, the wholesaler, find great investment deals and bring them to investors, and then you make money when you upcharge the price to the investor. For example, you find a property selling for $50,000 and you find a flipper willing to pay $55,000 for it. By dealing with the paperwork and acting as the go-between, you get to keep the difference between the two prices; that's your profit.

Seems easy enough, right?

Wholesaling is good in a lot of ways. It can teach amazing real estate investing skills such as numbers, deal-finding, negotiating, and networking. It also requires minimal to no money to start, so really anybody can do it. It can even be lucrative. While it's not always as easy to get into wholesaling as it's often advertised to be, it is a fairly simple process, and it's one you can do on your own time and with any amount of creativity you want to put into it.

But here's the reality check. Wholesaling is advertised as being an investment strategy. In no way whatsoever is wholesaling an investment strategy. Wholesaling is 100% work and 0% investment. Maybe you invest some dollars into making your fliers or advertising for properties or whatever, but that's purely an investment into your wholesaling *business*. Wholesaling is work. If you take up wholesaling, you've taken up a job. Taking on a new job is totally fine, as long as it's a job you were intending to take on. Down the road, you always have the option to create systems and processes around your wholesaling gig and hire people to do the work for you so you make it a passive venture, but all of that is still work. It's running a business. If you currently work 60 hours a week and have a family of five and you want to get into real estate investing, you need to understand that if you decide to wholesale that you're taking on a second job rather than investing, which may not be a realistic possibility with your already-full schedule.

Wholesaling can be a great way to build capital that you can invest into real estate, and it can teach you a heck of a lot about investing, but you can also build capital by taking on some other second job, getting loans, selling things on eBay, or starting a different kind of business; things that might be of more interest to you than wholesaling. I hate to burst the bubble of wholesaling being the easiest way for someone with no money to get started in investing, but it's just not investing.

chapter eight

Stop Managing Your Own Shit

One of the biggest misconceptions about real estate investing that often holds people back from investing for themselves is the thought that investing in real estate has to involve a lot of work. Or, as I've previously referred to it, hammer swinging.

As I said earlier, I was convinced when I first started looking into real estate that the only way to invest was to find motivated sellers, negotiate deals, rehab a property, place tenants, and then landlord those tenants. It wasn't that I couldn't do any of those things, but the thought of each one sounded miserable to me. Looking back, I know that's exactly why I didn't get into real estate initially—I didn't want to do any of that. It wasn't until I found alternative ways to invest that I finally jumped into becoming an investor. Those alternative ways were much more hands-off.

To give you some context as to how more hands-off investing can work, I'm going to compare two different approaches to rental property investing. I'll first explain the different approaches, and then we can debate which is the better option.

Traditional Rental Property Investing

The traditional way to invest in rental properties is called investing in a "value-add" deal. It's now more frequently referred to as the "BRRRR model", with BRRRR standing for *buy-rehab-rent-refi-nance-repeat*. These are the deals where you're buying a distressed property and then rehabbing it to increase the overall value of the property. When done correctly, the new value of the property since you improved it is now worth more than what you actually had to put into it. It's the same concept as flipping a property, but in these cases you're holding the property and renting it out rather than selling it at the higher value. But even if you hold it, that value you added is now added equity in the property and part of your overall profit.

In this method of buying rental properties, the process would go something like:

1. *Find a property.* You can find properties from many different sources. You might work with wholesalers, you might scour the MLS on a daily basis to catch a good deal as soon as it pops up, you might call property owners to see if they're interested in selling... it requires being creative sometimes.

2. *Negotiate the deal.* Once you find the deal you want, you have to work with the agent or wholesaler to get all the ducks in a row to close the deal.

3. *Close the deal.* This requires working with your lender, getting a property inspection completed, and finishing all the other appropriate due diligence items.

4. *Rehab the property.* Start swinging those hammers!

5. *Find tenants.* You have to advertise for tenants and then run applications as you get them, and eventually sign a contract with them and help them get moved in.

6. *Landlord the property.* You're taking maintenance (and drama) calls and either fixing issues yourself or hiring contractors to fix them. You stay up on current rent-

al property laws for your area and make sure you're in compliance with them. Ultimately, you're managing both the tenant and the property itself. And if a tenant needs eviction, you head up that process.

Turnkey Rental Property Investing

The idea behind a turnkey rental property, and where the name comes from, is that all you have to do [metaphorically] is stick the key in the door, turn it, and you're making cash flow immediately. This would imply the property is rent-ready, meaning no rehab required, and tenants are already secured and paying rent.

While the term 'turnkey' (also spelled 'turn key' and 'turn-key') technically refers to the condition of a property, oftentimes when people are referring to investing in turnkey rental properties, they're buying these properties from actual turnkey companies. These companies, also known as turnkey providers, go out and find distressed properties, buy them and rehab them, place tenants in them, and set up property management to manage the properties once they're purchased by the investor. Essentially, they're doing all of the "value-add" work mentioned above. This means that I, as the investor, am not the one doing all of that work. Instead, my investing process would look something like this:

1. *Select a property I like.* The turnkey providers give me a list of available inventory and I select which property I want.

2. *Sign the contract.* Sign and send it back to them.

3. *Do due diligence.* The most important step—to verify I'm getting the property as advertised. The most important things are to get a property inspection and verify all of the numbers.

4. *Close on the property.* Sign the closing documents.

5. *Manage the property manager.* This is minimal—it's just about keeping an eye out that the property is performing as expected. The worst case possibility in terms of effort is I may need to fire the property manager if they aren't performing and hire a new one, but I still never have to go in and fix a toilet or talk to a tenant.

Do you see a significant difference in workloads between the two scenarios? The lists may look to be of similar length, but how extensive each of those steps is varies greatly between the two approaches. The intensity of the workload of the traditional model is significantly more extreme than that of the turnkey method.

Based on those descriptions, you might be asking why anyone would do all the hard work if they can just go the turnkey route and have it all done for them.

It's all in the numbers.

Traditional vs. Turnkey: the Numbers

With residential real estate, "market value" is the perceived value of a property based on the market (things like current supply and demand and comps of similar properties). Using market value to compare the traditional and turnkey approaches:

Traditional approach: buy property significantly cheaper than market value then rehab the property—these two expenses should total less than the market value of the finished/improved property

Turnkey approach: buy finished/improved property at market value or close to it

In the traditional approach, you're forcing appreciation by improving (rehabbing) the property. Forcing appreciation means you find a distressed property, improve it in some way, and suddenly it's worth more than what you had to spend to fix it up. That additional value is now equity in your pocket, and you got that by 'forcing appreciation'.

For example, you buy a distressed property for $50,000 and you put $20,000 into the rehab on it, meaning you're $70,000 into the property. After the rehab, the property is now worth $100,000. That's an additional $30,000 of free equity that now belongs to you because you forced that appreciation via that rehab.

With a turnkey property, you're paying around market value for it and the property is already "improved", so you couldn't really improve the property if you wanted to. Even if you could, you'd have a hard time selling it for much more than market value anyway. With a distressed property, because you're buying it so far under market value, you have the room to do the rehab, force that appreciation, and sell it at the then-market value while still being able to keep profits in your pocket.

So then doesn't doing it all yourself sound like the better option then? The numbers are noticeably better with the traditional method than with the turnkeys, so why would anyone buy a turnkey over putting work into a property themselves?

Now we get to the meat of this conversation.

Pay More to Do Less Work, or Increase Returns by Doing More Work?

More often than not, people in this debate are in favor of increasing returns by doing the work themselves. There's a reason people insist this is the best way to succeed in real estate investing—it works. It doesn't mean though that hands-off methods don't work.

The most popular argument against turnkey is that you save money by doing everything yourself. This shows up in two primary areas when it comes to rental properties: saving money on the property purchase itself by being able to buy the distressed property well under market value, and saving money by landlording the property yourself instead of paying a property manager to do it for you. Are you really saving money by doing those things yourself, though? It depends on how you look at it.

Let's use property management fees to look at this. Typically a property manager charges the property owner 10% of the monthly rent as their fee for managing the property. So if your rental property brings in $1,000/month in rental income, the property management fee would be $100/month. When it comes to monthly cash flow, every $100 matters because usually you're only getting a couple to a few hundred per month. So it makes sense that people think they'd like to save this $100/month by just landlording themselves.

If landlording is easy or enjoyable for you and doesn't take away from your happiness in any way, then there's no reason to hire a property manager and you can pocket that $100/month. However, there are some considerations investors should ask when deciding whether to be a landlord:

- What is your personal time worth?
- How much time and work actually go into landlording?

Let's say I value my time at $75/hour. Meaning, if I were to do work for someone, I would charge them a rate of $75/hour. If a property manager charges me $100/month to do the landlording for me, how does this compare to the value of my time?

If I'm worth $75/hour, I would have to work 1.34 hours to make $100. If I were to spend 1.34 hours per month landlording my rental property, that would cost me the same as it would if I were to pay the property manager. If I spent less than 1.34 hours a month doing landlord duties, it means it would cost me less than $100, which means it would be financially advantageous for me to be the landlord. But if landlording took up more than 1.34 hours of my time per month, meaning more than $100 worth of my time, it would be more financially advantageous to pay the property manager $100 and not do the work myself.

Does it take more than 1.34 hours per month to landlord a property? Well, that depends on the property and the tenants. Do you have a low-end property that needs a lot of repairs or lower-quality tenants who are constantly needing something or breaking something or not paying rent? Or do you have low-maintenance properties and low-maintenance tenants and the overall time required to maintain them is minimal? Remember, too, that some months may require zero hours of your time while other months may require several hours. What will the average time be?

Here's a true story that happened on one of my properties. When I was involved in real estate investing in Nicaragua, I was traveling there often. I had also started buying rental properties by then, all of which were being managed by property managers. One afternoon I was sitting in the resort pool with a piña colada in my hand (I admit it wasn't the first one of the day) when I got a message from my property manager in Atlanta saying a storm had just blown through and taken off part of the roof of one of my properties. I told him to stand by while I called my insurance company. I called the insurance company, piña colada still in hand, initiated the claim and gave them my property manager's contact information so their adjuster could call him to coordinate the site visit to assess the damage. I hung up with them, shot my property manager a message back saying the claim was filed and the adjuster would be calling him. He said thanks, and that was the end of the conversation. Except for approving the final work order, I never did another thing about that roof because the property manager handled all of it with the insurance company and the contractors.

A storm blew the roof off my house, and I never once had to get out of the pool or put down my piña colada. If I had been the landlord on that property, I'm not even sure exactly what that would have done to my vacation at that moment. I don't know if I'd have hopped on a plane right then or if I could've hired someone from afar to go take a look at it. But I do know that, at a minimum, my task list associated with the roof would've been something like:

- communicate with tenants regarding temporary solutions and then again when the contractors would be working

- coordinate with the insurance adjuster

- meet the insurance adjuster at the property

- find a contractor for the work

- supervise the contractor who completed the work

How many hours would this have taken in total? I have no idea. But I do know that it adds up to significantly more than the five minutes it took me in the pool to get all of that work coordinated.

There's another consideration tied into all of this as well, aside from trading my time for money. What about that third currency—sanity? Never mind how much time I would've had to spend to deal with the roof of this property, and getting out of Nicaragua to do it, but compare the stress levels of dealing with all of that versus staying in the pool and not having to worry about it.

I know that the detriment to my sanity levels when I'm landlording is not at all worth me keeping an extra $100/month in my bank account. Some people, though, don't mind landlording duties and feel the work is worth keeping the extra $100 in their bank accounts each month with no psychological impact. This will be the same for comparing broader investing strategies as well—some people don't mind doing all the work and may even enjoy it, while other people won't like it at all. It's not about which route you choose, it's about understanding the different options and knowing which one is a best fit for you. Every investor needs to weigh the monetary logistics and the quality of life logistics for themselves as every investor and every situation will be different.

The thing is—most people don't realize there are ways to still be an investor without having to do so much work. It's conveniently something left out of all those how-to guides.

There are also some other considerations to think about when it comes to deciding whether or not you want to be the one doing all of the work for your properties or not.

Quality Isn't the Name of the Game Anymore

A lot of people come in with the argument that the only way to uphold the quality of your property is to do it all yourself. I don't disagree with this, but when you start thinking in these terms, you start teetering on the edge of creating an emotional attachment to your property. You should never have an emotional component in your investment properties. I know that's easier said than done; I've been guilty of it a time or two myself.

The reality is that not every property should be kept to the same levels you would keep your own house. If you're doing high-end rentals, maybe. But most rental properties aren't that nice. I've worked with deals in the past that were located in areas such that you would never get the highest-end tenants, so it would've been overkill to deck out the property with high-end materials. You wouldn't be able to charge more rent for the property anyway because market values only let you go so high, so it makes more sense to match the quality of materials to the neighborhood the property is in and the tenant quality. In no way is that to condone slumlording, but it just doesn't make sense to keep C- or B- grade properties at A-grade quality.

I know myself. If I were to landlord my rental properties, I would be fastidious about keeping them at the standard I'm used to. Meaning, I'd keep all my properties A-grade, regardless of the practicality of doing so. By using a property manager and letting him be in charge, I don't have to stress about the materials or the property not being at full A-grade all the time because I don't even have to see the properties. The properties are still kept in very nice condition, but I don't have to stress over things like rental-grade carpet versus luxury-grade and which one I think is better.

How much time and sanity would it cost you to keep a property at the exact standard you prefer? Now compare that to the level of reward you would get for doing so. For me, while I'd love for every one of my properties to be at the highest quality possible, the amount of dedication and effort it would take for me to get them to that level just isn't worth my stressing over it. Plus, it's not a one-time effort—it's one thing to get them to that high of a standard, but then you have to constantly maintain them at that level.

Having a property manager manage my properties alleviates me from having to micromanage the quality of my properties from the 'out of sight, out of mind' perspective. A lot of people may drop into a tailspin at the thought of not seeing their properties and being able to see the exact condition they're in, but for me it makes everything easier and less stressful to not worry about.

You Will Have to Trust Other People

When you let other people do the work for you, you have to trust those people. The less work you do, the more work someone else has to do for you, and that means the more people you will have to trust. A lot of people have no confidence in others and struggle to trust them. If you will lose sleep trusting other people to take care of your property or do work on your behalf, plan to run things yourself.

For those of us who are okay trusting other people, we can't expect that things will always go perfectly or that the people we trust today might not become untrustworthy later. Things happen, and you have to weigh the pros and cons of trusting other people to do your work, knowing they may falter or screw you over sometimes, and doing all of the work yourself. I've been screwed a time or two (or maybe three) by relying on other people. That's a reality you'll have to face. But I'd still choose getting screwed over a few times if it prevents the trouble of doing all the work myself.

Consider an Entrepreneurial Approach

This all leads to a bigger concept, which is entrepreneurship. Let's say you're going to start a business. You make the best pizzas on the planet, so people have encouraged you to start a pizza business. There are two options for how this business goes after the initial set up.

Option one: You're the primary person making the pizzas. If you go on vacation, pizzas don't get made. Therefore, you make no income. Your physical presence directly impacts the earnings.

Option two: You establish systems and procedures for your pizza company in such a way that anyone could make the same pizza you make. By doing this, you can remove yourself from the equation and insert employees in your place. When you go on vacation, sales aren't impacted at all. This strategy is exactly how franchises work. The original pizza makers and burger flippers are not required to do the work themselves to earn income.

These two options for how you could run a pizza business are exactly the same for how you can set up your real estate investing—you can do all of the work yourself or you can have people do it for you. Which route you choose for your real estate investing goes back to the conversation earlier about strengthening your strengths and following what's natural for you. If you're more technically-inclined, maybe you'd be best at doing the work yourself. If you're less technically-inclined and more about the bigger picture, managing a team of people to do the work for you might be the better bet.

This idea can be applied in two ways: deciding on the initial strategy you want to pursue, and thinking about how to structure your strategy choice. If you don't want to do anything technical, you can choose an investing strategy from the start that is less technically-inclined. If you're okay with more technical work, you can choose a more technical strategy, but you also have the option later to restructure that same strategy in such a way that it allows you to move out of the technical side and more into the bigger picture side.

Robert Kiyosaki explains a lot in his books about the difference of being a business owner and an employee. The difference between those two job roles is—outsourcing. When you agree to outsource parts of the business, meaning you hire someone else to do them, you begin to free yourself from having to do all of the active work yourself. That is the entrepreneurial approach—learning to become a business owner instead of resigning yourself to being an employee who does all of the work.

You Don't Need to Know How to Landlord to Manage a Landlord

Related to the idea of outsourcing jobs is the common misunderstanding that you should always landlord your own property first, even if you plan to switch to using a property manager. The reason people say you should do this is so that you can better understand how to manage the property manager. They're assuming that with firsthand experience as a landlord, you would know more about what you want out of a property manager and you'd understand their daily tasks, so you would be aware of whether or not they're doing their job correctly.

This would be true if it were an apples-to-apples comparison. Unfortunately, this is more of an apples-to-ham comparison. When you're landlording a property, you need to know things like: finding and managing tenants, taking maintenance calls and coordinating repairs, knowing and following state and local laws relevant to the property, filing and handling evictions, and being able to troubleshoot or problem-solve various things that may go on with the tenants or the property.

When you're managing a property manager, you only need to know how to manage the person who is doing all of those tasks. You don't personally have to know how to do any of those tasks; all you need to know is how to know if those tasks are getting done satisfactorily. Yes, someone could argue that you would need to know how to do those tasks so you would know what constitutes satisfactory, but as the property owner you can assume that if the income continues to come in, you see occasional property inspection documents ensuring the quality of the property is being maintained, and communication continues to flow with the property manager, you can probably assume those tasks are being completed satisfactorily.

Again, you don't need to know *how* those tasks are being completed, just that they are being completed. For example, you don't need to know the details of how to fix a toilet; you just need to know how to ensure the toilet gets fixed.

Knowing how to do the detailed, mundane, or smaller tasks of landlording will help you very little in managing a property manager because they are very separate things: managing technical tasks versus managing people.

Think back to owning and running a business. Imagine that instead of making pizzas, you buy a cupcake shop. You have no idea how to make cupcakes, and you're not interested in learning how. You might not even really know how to bake. But you, as the business owner, don't have to know how to make the cupcakes as long as you're capable of keeping people in place who do. There's a good chance these people know how to make cupcakes better than you ever could anyway. To keep the business thriving, your job is to consistently focus on the big picture, do the business duties, make sure all of your employees are functioning properly, and keep everything flowing smoothly. You don't necessarily have to know how to make a cupcake for that to happen.

Now think of the flipside of this scenario, where the town's best cupcake maker is encouraged to open their own cupcake shop. The most common reason a business like this fails is because the person who is so good at making cupcakes now has to run a business, which is a completely different skill set to making cupcakes. They aren't even in the same realm of skill sets. The cupcake master now loses their business or becomes miserable running it because the tasks of a business owner are completely different from those of a baker.

It goes both directions—business minds often don't thrive trying to do technical jobs, and technical minds can struggle with business tasks. Neither skill set is better or worse than the other, they're just different. People don't always see how skill sets differ and what roles are required, so they end up taking on something outside of their skill set without even knowing it.

There are, however, successful cupcake business owners who are great at making cupcakes so they bake most of the cupcakes for their shop. This is like the situation I mentioned earlier where the owner must be present to generate income. This would be the equivalent of landlording your own property. You are the business owner (investor), but you are skilled at doing the technical work (landlording), so you do it yourself and don't have to bring on someone else to help you.

If your intention is to one day run a cupcake empire, however, and your focus is the business and not baking cupcakes, you need to focus on learning how to manage the people and the players that make up your empire. Knowing how to make a good cupcake won't help you build that empire or keep it running because you won't have the time or capacity to build the empire if you're busy making cupcakes.

If you enjoy landlording your own properties and aren't necessarily trying to scale your portfolio, then learning how to landlord a property is what you should do. You can always switch to using property managers at some point in the future if you want to; you aren't tied to staying with one option or the other. But if your goal is never to be a landlord and you're more focused on having an empire, then learning to take maintenance calls and evict a tenant doesn't prepare you to build and run that empire.

What skills do you need to learn then? Well, that depends on your long-term goal. You're more than welcome to learn landlording tasks if you want to learn them or if you want to just be the landlord yourself for a while. But in no way is learning landlording tasks a requirement for knowing how to manage property managers. Not only is it not a requirement, but it's also an unrelated skill set.

Expansion Will Always Be Limited

It's not just the need to learn broader business skills that are necessary to build an empire, but to build an empire you also need the ability to grow.

If you flip properties and you do most of the work yourself, you can only flip so many properties at a time. But if you have a crew of people helping you in the various aspects of the flip, you can do several projects at once. Same if you're landlording; you can only landlord so many properties by yourself. If you want more properties than what you can landlord by yourself, you'll have to hire people to help you.

When you do all the work yourself, you limit how much can be done at one time.

I think back to when I was an engineer working in a corporate setting. If I was a one-person operation, I could only do so many engineering jobs at once. But if I moved to a management role and hired engineers to help work my projects, I could take on a number of engineering projects and would be limited only by how many people I have working for me.

If you aren't trying to become an empire-owning baller and you enjoy doing the projects yourself, there's nothing wrong with that. It's about knowing the limitations and whether those limitations will keep you from something you are trying to achieve. If you want to grow but you're unwilling to stop trying to manage everything yourself, how far you can grow will be limited.

Don't Be a Control Freak

If you are unwilling to stop trying to manage everything yourself, you might have issues with control.

Many of us have a compulsion to do everything ourselves. There are numerous reasons why you shouldn't do everything yourself, but sometimes what makes sense on paper doesn't make sense to our psyches. Or, I'll just say it, to our egos.

You can argue all day long that doing all the work yourself is the only good and safe way to do something. The problem comes in when you don't actually want to do all the work yourself, but you're catching yourself not being willing to release any of the control.

If you want to invest in more properties but you're unable to due to lack of resources—you're out of money or you don't have enough time—you should consider the possibility that you're being a control freak. I can say that, because I used to be one. Once you acknowledge the possibility you're being a control freak, you can give yourself permission to start considering doing things differently.

It's not about whether or not you decide to manage your investments yourself. The important thing to know is that there are options to not manage everything yourself. When you get into a situation where you wish you could invest in more properties but you find yourself out of resources to do that, you have to learn to release control and begin to outsource parts of your investing. Outsourcing is a different skill than managing the more technical aspects of properties, but it's a skill that will ultimately let you expand past your current inventory of resources.

At the end of the day, it's about assessing whether or not you really want to have to put that piña colada down when something goes astray on one of your properties.

chapter nine

What It Takes to Go Big

Now that you've considered shifting your mindset about some of the most foundational ideas in real estate investing, it's time to think about what it actually takes to go big as a real estate investor. Mind you, not every real estate investor wants to make it big. Not everyone wants a career in real estate, or an empire, or anything more than just a smart place to invest some money. Even if you're only interested in real estate investing on a smaller scale, understanding these concepts may still help you along your journey. On the other hand, if building an empire is your goal, it's imperative you know these concepts.

Leveraging

You already know that leveraging other people's money can increase the returns on an investment property. If you want to make it big as an investor, you're probably looking to maximize your returns, and leveraging becomes the obvious choice for accomplishing that.

The only way to make a mountain out of a molehill financially with investing is through leveraging. If you have $100 or $1,000,000 to invest and you don't leverage any of that money, you will be out of money to invest once you've spent it all. You either end up with $100 or $1,000,000 worth of assets. When you leverage, on the other hand, there's no cap on the amount of assets you can acquire. That $100 could get you $1,000,000 worth of assets if you get really creative with it.

If you do have $1,000,000 lying around that you can invest with, you might be able to make it big without leveraging any of it (depending on how big you're trying to get). But for most of us, you're going to need to consider leveraging as a means to making it big.

Think of leveraging as a means of getting past limitation. If you only have that $100 of investable cash, you're limited to just that $100. But leveraging and getting past limitation isn't just applicable to money. There are other things you can leverage.

Think about it in terms of limitation. What other than money are you limited on? Time and sanity, the other two currencies, are definitely limited. What else? Think about a soccer team. Can you play all of the positions on a soccer team by yourself? There's a reason there are multiple people on a soccer team and they are all playing different positions—all of those positions need to be covered, and in having multiple position options, everyone can play the position they are best at. When everyone is doing that, the team is operating at max capacity.

How are your brain and the real estate investing industry any different than the people on the team playing the soccer game? You can't cover all the positions on the field by yourself in real estate and operate at max capacity. So why not think about taking advantage of:

- other people's <u>expertise</u>
- other people's <u>knowledge</u>
- other people's <u>resources</u>
- other people's <u>mistakes</u>

Just like having a finite amount of money available for investing, you have finite skills, resources, and brain power. You may have a lot of all of those, but you're still only going to be able to operate at a limited capacity if you choose not to leverage the skills, resources, and brain power of others while trying to build an empire.

Leveraging other people's money can increase investment returns, but leveraging other people's knowledge and resources allows you to expand what's possible for your portfolio because now you have added skills, resources, and brain power. You might even be able to expand to levels you didn't even realize are attainable.

Without leveraging, you're limited. And there's no way to build an empire if you're constrained with limitation.

Outsourcing

In thinking of leveraging other people, this brings up a critical conversation that people of all industries should understand, not just real estate investors.

Many investors and entrepreneurs want to do everything themselves. It makes sense. You know how you want things done. You want to save the money you'd be paying someone else to do it. You wouldn't like how they do it anyway. And most of us have a little (or a big) control freak in us that we don't want to let go. But if you want to build an empire, you're going to have to shift your mentality about this.

When I started my company, Hipster Investments, I had a profound experience that taught me the real weight of the concept of valuing my time. As a brand new ~~control freak~~ entrepreneur, I was designing the company's website on my own. I had never been great at super techy stuff (despite being an engineer), but I knew enough to create a basic website, plus I loved design. So, part of me doing the website myself was that I loved designing it, but the bigger part of it was that I didn't want to pay someone else to do it.

I had the site up and running pretty well, but one innocent Friday afternoon I hit a snag. I don't remember it in detail, but it was a very small problem in the bigger scheme of things. But still, it had to be fixed. I signaled my engineering brain and went into problem-solving mode. <u>Seven hours later</u>, still in problem-solving mode and now cross-eyed from having stared at the computer for so long, things were looking bleak. It seemed as though I wasn't going to solve this thing by myself, but I hadn't given up. Out of curiosity, I reached out to a web guy I had recently met. I told him the problem I was having, and he said he would take a quick look. Within 1.5 minutes (90 seconds), he had fixed the problem. It literally took him under two minutes.

Now put some perspective on this. Say I'm worth $100/hour (I gave myself a raise from my previous $75/hour). If I just spent seven hours working on that computer problem, in theory I spent $700 working on that computer problem when I could have otherwise been working for my usual $100/hour. My web guy at the time was charging $12/hour. It took him 1.5 minutes to solve my computer problem, so I ended up paying him $0.30—1.5 minutes at a rate of $12/hour.

It cost me __30 cents__ to have a problem resolved that I spent $700 trying to fix myself.

How much is your time worth?

No empire-owner does everything themselves. Not only is it impossible to do from a time perspective, but it's not cost-effective. If you keep your real estate investing ventures as a side thing, or you just enjoy doing the work, you can certainly continue to do everything yourself. But if you want to build the empire, hiring help is non-negotiable. This is called outsourcing. At initial glance, it seems like paying someone to do work that you could do yourself costs you money. But depending on the work and what's required for it to be done, and your skill level, outsourcing may actually save you money.

Outsourcing not only can save you money, but then you're also going back to the idea of utilizing other people's expertise and knowledge—some of the aforementioned leveraging points—which means that they can get the job done better than you can anyway.

Allowing yourself to consider the value of your time opens the door to outsourcing, which ultimately leads to a tremendous opportunity in building your empire bigger than you ever thought possible.

Mobility

Things are always changing. Life is always changing. Real estate deals and markets are always changing. The best deals today are unlikely to be the best deals in a year or five years from now.

One nice thing about the real estate investing industry is the fluidity of it. The fluidity can be frustrating if you aren't sure how to best use it in your favor, but if you're willing to go with it, you'll be able to maximize your returns. And if you want to make it big, maximizing returns is probably in the forefront of your thoughts.

A basic example of the fluidity of real estate is looking at the peaks and the crashes of the real estate market. The peaks are when prices are at their highest, and a crash is the same as a recession and is when prices are at their lowest. The real estate market operates on a cycle—it's constantly fluctuating between peaks and crashes. One way of being fluid with real estate would be acknowledging that different real estate investing strategies should be used at different times during the real estate market cycle. What's most advantageous during a peak is likely the opposite of what would be most advantageous during a crash. Knowing which strategy is most effective at what point in the market cycle, and being willing to pursue those strategies at their appropriate times, will allow you to maximize your returns.

This represents mobility as a real estate investor—the willingness to shift your strategy as needed based on the current conditions and what would be most advantageous for your bottom line in that moment.

In addition to using the right strategy at the right time in the real estate market cycle, knowing *where* to get the most advantageous deals is also ever-changing. This represents physical mobility. For example, quite often in a recession, certain cities will offer extremely profitable returns. When this happens, investors go screaming into those cities and buy like crazy. Because of that sudden influx of demand, prices eventually start to soar. As a result, returns shrink and inventory becomes low. At that point, those cities are no longer the most advantageous cities for investment returns. Just like the general real estate market experiencing a cycle of ups and downs, cities can experience the same thing.

Being willing to be physically mobile with your investing, so that you can always invest in the most advantageous locations based on where they are in their own market cycles, is another way of using mobility to help you maximize your returns.

If you do want to build that empire, you have to be willing to look at the bigger picture of how and where to get the highest returns. Otherwise, if you aren't willing to be mobile and adjust to the ever-changing real estate climates, your growth and your bottom line will always be limited.

Perseverance

Remember those big-time investors who have failed several times? The difference between those who make it big and those who don't is perseverance. Perseverance through the challenges. Perseverance through the failures. Perseverance in learning. Perseverance in making things happen. Other words you could use would be persistence, tenacity, determination, insistence, and drive. No one builds an empire without embracing these virtues.

Perseverance can feel brutal at times, but it's when you have the cojones to barrel through that you will really begin to see success.

chapter ten

How to Never Succeed

We've already talked about how to soften your journey into real estate investing using tactics like focusing on your strengths, following what comes naturally to you, and being strategic in figuring out which real estate investing route might be the best fit for your goals. But what about the last piece of the mindset puzzle: what's it really going to take to succeed?

One of the easiest ways to discover what it'll take for you to succeed is to tell you what *not* to do. If you can avoid the following mistakes, you're much more likely to get to where you want to go, and hopefully with fewer headaches along the way.

Mistake: Investing with Minimal Education Under Your Belt

There's a reason no toddler is thrown into a swimming pool without floaties and a chaperone. They would drown. Similarly, if you dive into real estate investing without having taken any swim lessons, you will drown too. Also, you can't learn how to swim with just one lesson.

The truth is, like with most things in life, slow and steady really does win the race. It's especially important when it comes to gaining an education in real estate investing. Taking the time to get some foundational knowledge under your belt is imperative. If you don't build a solid foundation, you could risk everything by putting it into a totally bunk investment.

It doesn't take much time to learn the basics. You should never be in such a rush that you miss out on getting foundational knowledge.

It only takes a little education to be significantly more prepared and to make safer investments. If I were to pick the most important essentials of real estate investing that every investor needs to understand, they would be:

- differences in investing strategies and how each strategy relates to particular goals
- risks of each strategy and how to mitigate those risk factors
- how to run the numbers
- market/city analyses

That's a very short list and can be learned fairly quickly. If you take the time to learn each of these four things, you will have set yourself miles ahead of most other people getting involved in real estate investing and you're likely to succeed more quickly as a result. It doesn't mean you won't ever fail, but you're at least lessening your chances of failing or lessening the degree of failure.

Mistake: Believing Everything You Read

Let's just be frank. Most people are idiots. And if you start taking advice from those idiots, you're going to be in for a world of hurt.

I think we have a serious TMI (too much information) problem these days. The internet is great—it provides vast amounts of information and makes our lives significantly easier. But in many ways, it can make life harder as well. How do you know that what you're reading on the internet or hearing people say is true? You don't. Today more than ever, you have to learn to decipher information for yourself.

Following the advice of people who are successfully doing what you want to do is the first step in deciphering what information you need to listen to. You can probably trust that most of what they tell you is valid since they are succeeding themselves. But if you're in an online forum where there are literally no checks and balances to who is speaking or what is said, be cautious. The most ignorant and unsuccessful person can make themselves sound like an expert online when they're actually giving false and misleading information.

Mistake: Listening to Everybody Around You

Have I mentioned there are a lot of voices out there? Not only will listening to everyone around you likely cause you to lose sanity, but you're probably going to take on some really bad advice at some point.

I don't know if you've noticed, but the people around us tend to have a lot of opinions about other people's lives. I actually think it's yet another rite of passage for investors to run into a million people trying to tell them what a bad idea it is to get into real estate investing.

While I think it's always a good idea to at least hear and consider all of the advice that comes your way, because you never know what piece of advice will be the real ticket to your success, I'm also a huge advocate of considering the source from which the advice is coming from. With that in mind, I want to share with you the most powerful idea I have lived by throughout my real estate and entrepreneurship careers:

Don't take advice from someone you wouldn't trade shoes with.[9]

---

9   I haven't been able to pinpoint where I came up with this phrase in order to be able to give credit to who said it initially. Hopefully I created it myself and am not plagiarizing it.

One of the best examples of using this quote to help me decide who I should be taking advice from comes from my experience with my own family as I was trying to get into investing. My dad was always the kind to get up early, work hard, save every penny he could, and invest conservatively. He worked a ton and was very frugal. His sister, my aunt, was the opposite. She was always an investor, spent her money freely, and took chances. Both of their paths led them to great financial success. As I started getting curious about investing, I brought it up to both of them and suddenly I was getting advice from both of them. The problem was, each person's advice contradicted the advice of the other. So who was I supposed to listen to?

When I compared the life I wanted to live to both my dad's life and my aunt's life, my vision more strongly resembled the way my aunt went about things. While my dad is one of my favorite people on the planet, I've never wanted to stringently work for someone else and save every penny I earn. So when I started thinking about investing, I listened to my aunt over my dad. I listen to my dad for a million other things in life but not investing. Why? Because I've never wanted to trade shoes with him in that arena. I would, however, trade shoes with my aunt in the investing department. So, I chose to take advice from the person I wanted to trade shoes with because that seemed to make the most sense.

Another example of when this quote played a critical role in my life was when it came to me becoming an entrepreneur. When I first was curious about real estate investing, which later led to me starting my business, I met someone during a contract meeting who was living what I perceived to be the dream life. He had his own company, could work whatever hours he wanted, and he could travel anytime he wanted. He was demonstrating a lifestyle design nearly identical to what I wanted for myself. For these reasons, I always listened to every piece of advice he ever offered me, and doing so eventually led me to start a business that allowed me all of the same luxuries he had. I would trade shoes with him, so I listened to him. The contrast to that would've been to take advice on how to live my dream life of freedom from a guy wearing a suit sitting behind a desk Monday through Friday 9-to-5. Wouldn't make much sense, would it?

Mistake: Expecting Someone to Tell You How to Do Everything

First of all, no one who actually knows what they're doing is going to have enough time on their hands to do everything for you or tell you how to do it all. Second, it's rude to ask. But more importantly, it's not the way to find the greatest level of success.

You are your own person. Your success will come from something that is uniquely yours. It's unlikely that exactly what worked for someone else will work in the same way for you. The premise of what you do in investing and business may be the same as someone else's, but how you actually make it happen has to be unique to you in order to satisfy your own strengths and interests. Trying to replicate exactly what someone else does is like saying you should adopt a particular personality to succeed. It's just not possible to do that, and why would you want to? No two people are going to have the same path to success.

You can, however, adopt ideas and practices from multiple sources and add your own flare. Don't take that to mean you have to make your process overly complicated and find different pieces all over the place and piece them together, but just understand that success comes when you learn various pieces as you go and combine them into a system that works for you.

If you find a mentor, whether in person or through reading books, you can absolutely strive to replicate their processes. But be open along the way to learning additional tools that might be specific to your own personal success.

Mistake: Trusting What People Tell You

Not only do you have to be careful about what you read and who's giving you advice, but if you trust everything anyone tells you as a real estate investor, you're going to be in for a bumpy ride. There will be a million people trying to tell you what you should and shouldn't be doing (when really they have no idea what you should or shouldn't be doing), but more critically there will always be a seller trying to convince you why you should buy a particular investment property. If you don't have enough education and willingness to ultimately make decisions for yourself without basing them solely on what everyone tells you, your investments will be as good as toast.

Trust in this section is different than the trust talked about earlier in the **You Will Have to Trust Other People** section. There are different types of relationships within any industry. The earlier discussion speaks to the fact that you have to trust other people to help you on your journey if you want to experience any level of freedom. In order to not do everything yourself, you have to hire other people to take over certain tasks. This is when you have to learn to trust other people (with proper vetting, of course).

The trust I refer to in this section isn't about trusting someone to take care of certain tasks for you; it's about listening to what people say. If you're relying on what someone tells you about a deal, it means you haven't done the due diligence yourself. And if you aren't doing thorough due diligence on properties before you buy them, you're setting yourself up for a potential meteor to strike your investment career.

Know this: *there is very little that you can't verify about a real estate deal.*

For instance, if you're buying a rental property, verify to the best of your ability all of the projected numbers. Find out the property tax amount via the tax assessor's website, get an actual insurance quote, and ask more than one property manager or real estate agent who specializes in rentals what they estimate you can get in rent for that particular property. The only numbers you can't get actuals on are repairs and vacancies. If you're flipping or rehabbing properties, get a thorough property inspection done and one or two quotes to have the work done (and maybe add a 10% cushion for when the rehab inevitably goes over budget). Then you can do due diligence on things like the title on the property and other components that could cause problems. There are ways to verify just about everything about a property. The only things you can't verify or do due diligence on are unexpected things that may cause a freak situation that no one could've known about ahead of time.

Nowhere in any of that due diligence did you have to trust anything anybody told you; you verified everything for yourself. You want to be self-sustaining in the analysis part of investing. Sure, you can use other people as resources and get information from them, but at the end of the day, the decision to move forward on an investment or walk away should be yours and yours alone based on your own verification processes.

The only way to get to the position of being able to do thorough due diligence is with education. Education is how you can avoid relying on what people tell you and being able to know for yourself what you're getting into.

So, remember that you have to trust other people enough to take a step back and allow them to handle day-to-day tasks for you, but as far as your investing decisions, those should always only come from you, and you should have the proper education to make those decisions intelligently.

Mistake: Not Accepting Help

I know, I know—we're all geniuses and completely capable of succeeding in this world through our own volition. We're way too smart to need help from anyone, and no one else can do it better than us anyway. True? Sorry, but no matter who you are, no one can build an empire by themselves. It's just not possible to know all of the answers or to do everything ourselves.

At a minimum, if you try to do everything on your own, you will incessantly and unnecessarily keep reinventing the wheel. Maybe you occasionally come up with something ingenious that no one else has done before, but the other 99.5% of the tasks and processes have already been perfected by someone else. Don't be too proud to learn from someone who is operating a successful investment strategy. Letting other people help you and being willing to learn from other people will save you immense amounts of time and strain.

But of course, if you want to stick to your guns and do it all yourself, by all means, see if you can make E equal something other than mc^2.

Mistake: Not Trying Anything

Simple truth: you'll never accomplish anything if you don't do anything.

As I've said, you can't know every single thing you need to know for successful real estate investing without ever trying an investment. You probably won't know everything you need to know even after your first five investments. It's an ongoing learning curve, and you will only get better with time, experience, and learning from your mistakes. Therefore, you've got to try things at some point.

Mistake: Quitting After You Fail

You might as well just quit *before* you fail if all it's going to take to make you throw in the towel is some lost money. With successful real estate investing comes failing. There's no way around it. We're talking about an industry that:

- we learned nothing about in school
- primarily has to be self-taught
- can be done a million different ways
- has inevitable challenges
- requires creativity
- requires extensive problem-solving

How would someone ever be able to do all of that and not fail at least once? I dare you to find even one wildly successful investor who hasn't failed, and likely failed to the tune of millions of dollars.

How did they end up succeeding with all that failure? They didn't quit after they failed, that's how.

Mistake: Not Learning From Your Mistakes

Not learning from your mistakes is just as bad as quitting after you fail. It gets you nowhere, and it won't help your chances for investing success because success comes from learning from your mistakes. You can persist after a failure, but if you never learn what it was that caused the failure in the first place and you don't make changes to avoid that same failure again, you're not going to get anywhere. You're just setting yourself up for an obnoxious cycle of frustration.

Mistake: Being a Control Freak

Thinking you have control over much of anything in life is a joke. You can always control the effort you put into something, but you can rarely control the outcome. You can implement a lot of risk mitigation to prevent undesirable outcomes with an investment property, but you can't completely eliminate risk. So why pretend you can?

Being a control freak won't always cause problems, but it rarely helps anything. I already touched briefly on the possibility of someone being a control freak with their investing, but it's worth diving into just a little deeper and understanding more about the potential consequences of being a control freak in real estate investing.

Being a control freak can cause one or several of the following in real estate investing:

- never actually getting started
- missing out on the best deals
- not accepting the help required to succeed
- costing yourself more money
- not utilizing the expertise of people smarter than you
- missing out on leveraging advantages
- reinventing the wheel
- losing sanity
- losing sleep

Again, this comes down to an evaluation of how you rank your three currencies, along with your personal skill sets and interest levels. What one person may lose on a deal by being a control freak may be completely different from what another person loses. And maybe you only want to own a couple of properties that you do 100% of the work on, controlling every part of the process along the way, and that works for you. But in the bigger scheme of things, there's a good chance that trying to control every part of the process is going to hurt you more than it's going to help you. Ultimately, being a control freak all the time tends to have the reverse effect of success and expansion.

One thing to note is the difference between being a control freak and being *in control*. You do need to be in control as an investor. For example, if a tenant stops paying rent, you need to buck up and do whatever you can to prompt that payment. If you have a property manager managing your rental property and things aren't going quite right, you have to be able to stand up to the manager and force them to perform. If you're flipping a house and one of your contractors slacks off, you need to make some moves on him. All of those things require a necessary amount of control. Being a control freak means you're *overcontrolling* things.

It's all about balance—how to release control when you need to release control and how to take control when it's necessary for your investment. But staying in control the entire time and in all parts of the equation is only going to hold you back, gray your hair, and probably annoy everyone around you.

Mistake: Not Learning the Numbers

How does anyone expect to profit in an industry that is solely based on numbers if they have no idea how to run or analyze numbers?

Investing is math. Math is numbers. On any given investment, what are the numbers and what goes into the numbers? The profit is in the numbers. If you don't know where your profit is coming from, and you don't know how to run the math, you aren't going to get a profit.

What's the cash flow on the property? What's the after repair value (ARV)? What's the market value? What's your interest rate? What's the income? What are the expenses? What's the cap rate? What's the cash-on-cash return? What's the projected return on investment (ROI)? What's included in that particular ROI? By the way, people tend to include whatever they want in ROI projections, so be sure you know exactly what someone's projected ROI is based on to ensure accuracy. Which of the numbers are estimates versus actuals? What market and property elements contribute to whether the projected numbers actually play out as predicted? Where are things most likely to go wrong with the numbers?

If you don't know what these questions mean or how to answer them, you don't know enough yet about the numbers and how to analyze them. And if you don't understand the numbers, you're missing the biggest foundational piece of investing.

It may seem like this list of things not to do if you want to succeed in real estate investing is really intense, but it's actually not that bad. It just comes down to taking the time to get some foundational knowledge before you dive in and continuing to persevere no matter what happens along the way.

More often than not, fear is what prevents us from getting started or continuing past obstacles we hit along the way. Fear is a completely normal emotion because not only do you potentially have a lot of money riding on your success, but this is also a solo venture, so it's easy to tie any 'failures' into your self-worth. We feel these fears because we're human. The trick is to get past the fear. Do the opposite of everything on this list and you're bound to see some level of success down the road.

part four

How to Get Into the Pool Without Drowning

chapter eleven

Getting Started

Here's the tricky part about getting started. You don't want to get started with little or no education about real estate investing under your belt. However, you also don't want to wait so long while you're getting all that education that you end up never doing a deal. There's no way to avoid mistakes, but it is possible to (hopefully) avoid detrimental mistakes. The trick is finding the balance between having enough education and being willing to dive in.

I know I've been pretty adamant about not giving you any actual how-to guides, but—sneak attack— I'm going to give you one.

While this isn't a technical how-to guide for any particular real estate investing strategy, it is a how-to guide to help you get started as a real estate investor (or anything in life, for that matter). This is literally the exact process I followed as I tried to find my way out of my corporate engineering job. When I started this process I wasn't specifically trying to pursue real estate investing—I was trying to find my way out of my corporate job. It was in the middle of this process that I landed on real estate investing. For you though, you may already know you want to be a real estate investor and you use this process to get you settled into the industry. Either way, these are tried and true steps for getting you whatever it is you want to get involved with.

The idea with this process is to help you find the balance between having enough education to get you started safely but not spending too much time over-educating yourself to the point you never get started. Another factor that's built into this is… going way back to **Chapter Six: Don't Shave Years off Your Life**… finding out where your strengths are, as well as what things may come natural to you. I still stand by the idea that if you can figure out the things that are in your natural grain, you will have exponentially more success than if you fight uphill for skills you may not be as naturally inclined for.

One last caveat about the process I'm going to offer you is that you should remember none of it is set in stone. The best way to follow any process in life is to set your intentions for that process and plan to follow it, but while also being open to any deviations that may come up that could send you in a more productive direction. Deviations are very different than distractions, so be careful to not confuse the two. Don't follow just any shiny object that tries to deter you from your plan, but always be open to the idea that there may be a better solution out there than what you think will be the one.

And now that your suspense is in full swing, grab your pen and write down these steps. I'll list them here, and then I'll expand on each of them in the chapters to follow.

Step 1: Decide what you want

Step 2: Explore

Step 3: Choose your focus

Step 4: Study up

Step 5: Make a move

Step 6: Learn and continue

Seem overly simple? Well, they are simple. A solid foundation of any sort is often going to come from the most simple of ideas. The whole idea of these steps is to build as solid of a foundation for yourself as possible so that you not only avoid overly costly mistakes, but also to help you find the investing path that may be most successful for you.

While simple, I'll expand on each so you can get a firm understanding of exactly how to do them.

chapter twelve

Decide What You Want

Oddly enough, this seems to be the most commonly skipped step when people start getting into real estate investing. It should be obvious that someone would ask themselves why they want to become an investor before they set out to do it, but I think there's just an inherent knowing by most that being an investor can be very smart and lucrative, so people just assume they should do it and they don't question anything past that.

If being an investor is an obviously smart thing to do, why should anyone bother questioning why they want to do it? Answer: because understanding why you really want to do it will prove to be critical along the way. It will be critical for two reasons:

1. Understanding why you want to invest is directly related to your goals for investing, and understanding your goals will help you better choose the strategy that could be the best fit for you and bring you the highest potential for success.

2. When the going gets tough, which it will at some point, it's helpful to be very clear on exactly why you're doing it at all so that you will remain motivated to overcome the challenges and reach your goal.

If nothing else, understanding what it is you really want can give you a heck of a lot of motivation to want to really dive into this industry and make the journey into it a lot more exciting.

So how do you get clear on exactly what it is that you want out of being an investor? Money is an obvious answer for everyone, but money isn't going to be what clarifies a strategy for you or pushes you through the challenges. What's going to help you with both of those things is your *why*.

What is Your *Why?*

As with any venture in life, you'll always be the most effective if you determine your *why*. Why are you doing what you're doing? And I don't mean basic *why's* like financial security or even financial freedom (even though those are pretty powerful). *Why* do you want financial security or financial freedom? Dig deep! While you're thinking about it, I'll give you some scenarios to see what going deeper with your *why* looks like.

Let's say you want to become a flipper. Why do most people want to flip houses? Answer: to make a lot of money. Okay, that's valid. But why do you want to make so much money? The reason this matters is because—flipping can be hard. If you get into flipping properties and you begin to hit tough challenges (or failures) as you go along, you're going to have to have a really deep reason for wanting all that money to keep you going. If your *why* isn't that strong, there's a high likelihood that you may not persevere through the challenges.

Take this scenario: You grew up really poor. Your family was never really able to provide for you and because of that, you had a hard time getting through school and in some cases even being able to develop healthy relationships. Now you're an adult and you have children of your own. Because of your own experiences and knowing what growing up poor and not-provided for felt like, you never want your kids to have to experience that. You know that flipping properties can provide for your family in a way that you were never provided for. This is your *why*—doing everything in your power for your kids to not have to experience what you went through.

If you then begin flipping properties, and maybe all goes well for a minute but then a major challenge arises, how motivated are you going to be to figure out how to overcome that challenge? If the livelihood of your entire family depends on whether or not you succeed, I'd say you're going to be pretty motivated! That *why* is a deep one; not only does your and your children's livelihood depend on you succeeding, which is huge in itself, but it's also an emotional healing for yourself and what you went through as a child.

I'll tell you my personal *why*. My *why* has always been freedom. One could argue that I'm obsessed with freedom. I want to do what I want to do, when I want to do it, and how I want to do it. I tell the story all the time about how I'm the one crazy person in Los Angeles, where traffic is usually exhaustively stop-and-go, who drives a stick-shift car. I drive a stick because I don't even want my transmission telling me what to do; I want to shift when I want to shift. I know that's a dramatic reach for freedom, but I told you one could argue I'm obsessive with it. I also just get bored driving, so having to shift gives me something to do. Another example is when I was a rookie on my college rugby team. As is standard with a lot of sports team, rookies tend to be given hell from the veteran players during their first year. It's the same as pledging a frat. Well you can imagine how well it went for the veterans getting what they wanted when they commanded me to do something; it basically didn't happen. After a while, the veterans figured out that it was pointless to tell me to do anything. Even today, there's a good chance if you tell me to do something, I'll either not do it or I'll do completely the opposite. I'm not a jerk about it, I'm respectful about it, and if you're in a legit authority position over me, I'll completely honor that. But otherwise, I make my own rules, which for me is freedom.

Freedom for me is about as strong of a *why* as someone could have. My happiness levels are directly correlated to how much freedom I have. If there's any place in my life that I'm under someone else's rule, and I don't want to be there, I will go into alert mode and do everything in my power to gain freedom in that area. Without such an intense drive for freedom, I wouldn't have survived entrepreneurship as long as I have. Entrepreneurship can be hell! Talk about an emotional and mental roller coaster. But in the worst of times, I knew I had no choice but to figure out how to get around the obstacle because if I didn't, my freedom would be at risk. If I ever had to go back to a regular job, I would have to work under someone else's rules, interests, goals, and schedules. Not one of those things constitutes freedom to me. In the challenging moments where I wonder whether or not I can continue on as an entrepreneur, I feel like I literally have no choice but to keep at it. That's how strong my *why* is—it gives me no choice but to persevere. This is how strong your *why* should feel for you.

Real estate investing isn't about the money. It's about what the money gets you. I've never heard of anyone who legitimately just wanted the money without there being an underlying reason for wanting that money. What are you going to do with the money once you get it?

- provide for your family or someone close to you
- allow yourself to retire early, which would allow you to _____ (fill in the blank)
- prove yourself to someone (which is always actually just yourself, but you may think it's your parents or anyone who may not have believed in you)
- spend time volunteering and giving back
- fund causes you're passionate about

Somewhere in one of those is likely your *why*. Mine falls under that retiring early option because retiring usually means freedom, and the lifestyle I want is exactly that of a retired person—no set schedule, I can do what I want, and I report to no one.

If you aren't sure yet exactly what your *why* is, a fun homework assignment is to ponder your *why.* Don't try to think specifically about your *why* though, but instead think about your ultimate desires. What are the most important things to you in your life and for your life? If you could have anything you wanted, what would that be exactly? If you were creating a vision board for your life, what would be on it? Once you create that vision of all the things you want, look for a theme. What do all of those things have in common? Do they represent freedom, like they do in my case, or do they represent something like security? Or joy. Or status. Within all of those desires is your *why.* You may not figure out your *why* right away—sometimes our *why* can take years to truly know. But as long as you're keeping an eye out for it, you're going to better understand why you're doing all of this, which will ultimately help you toward greater success.

Putting Your *Why* to Use

Because there are so many different available strategies in real estate investing, it's critical that you know what you're driving toward. Not just to keep you motivated along the way, but to help you determine the right strategy for you. For example, knowing my *why* is freedom, I can know pretty quickly that wholesaling and flipping aren't the right strategies for me. Not only do both of those strategies require a lot of work, but I already said that what work they do require is not work I enjoy in any way. Nothing about any of that screams freedom to me. It makes sense in hindsight why I ended up with turnkey rental properties as my real estate investing strategy—they are about as hands-off as owning real property can be, which very much falls in line with my desire for freedom.

At this point, you don't have to know what strategies fit your *why*. What's important at this stage is to be aware of what your *why* is so that as you dive more into these next steps you can be cognizant of whether or not different options are congruent with your *why* or not. Your *why* can even change along the way, but the more connected you are with it from the start, the more efficiently you can tailor your real estate investing to whatever that is.

The important thing is to keep your *why* in the forefront of your mind as you start to explore your options.

chapter thirteen

Start Exploring

Now things get fun. Not only have you gone down the rabbit hole of envisioning your true dreams to help you determine your *why*, which is fun by itself, but now you get to start looking around and finding things to support your *why*. This is like injecting steroids into that vision board. Maybe not when you first start exploring, but it will definitely feel like a steroid injection the first time you find something that seems to support your epic desire!

The key for this step is to remember—you're not supposed to figure anything out yet. This step is really fun because there's no pressure whatsoever to come up with any answers.

Real estate investing is complicated partially because of how many different ways you can do it. There are a ton of different strategies you can do, and within each of those strategies are multiple ways you can do it. Adding that to the fact that we didn't learn anything about any of it in school, it really leaves a pretty big playground for learning and knowledge. I use the word "playground" intentionally to try to keep a feeling of positivity to it rather than a feeling of overwhelm.

There's no way to know your investing options if you don't know what's out there. This is where exploring comes in handy—you can begin to see what all exists. And once you start to see what exists, you can start to get a better handle on what of those things might be a fit for you.

When I was in the exploring phase, I was signing up for every webinar, every email list, and every cheap or free course I could. I especially loved reading actual books. My bookshelves got very filled up within the span of just a couple years. I was constantly reading a new book! With all of those resources, I really wasn't doing anything more than just taking it all in. I wasn't trying to make decisions, choose a path, or trying to immediately implement anything. I was just letting my brain receive a gigantic stockpile of information.

Once all of that information started filling my head, then I was able to start watching out for what was resonating with me. More than anything else, the idea of passive income was drawing me in. I was also really digging the concept of leveraging. Once I realized that passive income and leveraging were grabbing my attention to the degree that they were, I looked for more books and resources that would teach me more about these concepts.

One thing that helped me with looking for more information on these concepts was finding authors who were in support of them. Robert Kiyosaki, for example, is a huge supporter of passive income and leveraging. Because of this, if you look at my bookshelves today, you'll see a ton of books from his Rich Dad series. What you won't find on my bookshelves is any books from Dave Ramsey. Dave Ramsey has very solid financial principles, but they're in support of a different track from the one I resonate with.

This is how I began to narrow down a gigantically large playground of ideas and concepts—I found the things that were grabbing my attention and began to tailor my explorations to focus more on those topics, while exploring less on ideas or concepts that didn't resonate with me in the same way. Think of it like a funnel.

You start really broad with very little, if any, focus. Because there's so much information out there and so many different directions you can go as a real estate investor, the best thing you can do is to start by exploring all of the options out there. Read up on everything you can, go to a couple of workshops (cheaper ones, not $20,000 guru seminars), go to some local REIA meetings, and network with other investors. Check things out online, find some published real estate authors you like and read their books, and just start to get a feel for what's out there. Once you get some insight into the industry and the various options within it, you can start focusing on things that appeal to you. Maybe it's the writings of a particular author, or maybe it's a particular strategy or concept that seems appealing. Keep exploring those and continue to follow where your interests carry you.

As you begin to pick out things that resonate with you, you begin to get slim down your focus from extremely broad to slightly more focused. Then you begin to focus more, and then some more. Eventually you've got your sights on something that both interests you and supports your *why*.

Then it's time to move on from exploring and start to put some real work into your focus.

Side Bar: Guru Seminars

During this time of exploration, you're likely going to be running across a lot of invites to attend real estate investing workshops and seminars put on by various people in the industry. There are a lot of real estate investing "gurus" out there, and many of them charge significant amounts of money to attend their seminars. It's important to have a plan for navigating all of these offerings for two reasons:

1. So you don't get completely overwhelmed and confused by all of the information available in them and get frustrated with the industry before you've even had a chance to try it out.

2. So you don't spend an inordinate amount of money that ends up not helping you move forward as an investor.

While it's not the worst thing in the world to get more education than you should, it's helpful to be a little more tailored in your pursuit for education in terms of what education you get and from where. So the question becomes—should you do the guru seminars at all, and if so, when should you do them?

Are Guru Seminars Legit?

This is everyone's first question. Are guru seminars legit or are they a scam? And just when you're starting to convince yourself they're legit, you look online for more information and... ack, the bottom falls out.

If you look up any particular guru seminar online, you'll find that negative reviews run pretty rampant. It's the famous story of, "I paid $20,000 for a seminar on how to flip a house but it never worked and they kept my $20,000!" Or someone says they went to a seminar, perhaps paying much less than $20,000, but they couldn't get any information from it because the whole thing was just full of sales pitches so they were ripped off.

Argument: It didn't work!

There's no doubt that there are probably some 'gurus' out there running a scam. However, I don't think that's usually the case. I think the more common issue is that people pre-emptively sign up for an expensive seminar or program thinking that once they go their life/career/investing will be figured out for them, but they don't realize the level of effort they will have to put into implementing what they learn in order to be successful. Some people think paying $20,000 for the course or seminar *was* the heavy lifting and that, just by attending, they'll achieve the success they're looking for. Unfortunately, that $20,000 is just what it takes to open the door to begin the heavy lifting.

There is no overnight success in real estate investing. It takes a lot of work, a lot of effort, and a lot of perseverance through the challenges and failures. No amount of money will allow you to circumvent that process. And the bummer is that most people aren't willing to put in that kind of work. Then, when it doesn't turn out the way they think it's supposed to, they blame the guru or the seminar and write a horrible review. When all the while, all they are really doing is projecting their failure onto everyone else and refusing to hold themselves accountable for not putting the information they learned to work.

Argument: It was all sales pitches!

Just because a seminar presents you with persistent sales pitches doesn't mean the course is worthless or a scam.

The way the education profit funnel works for the people or companies who are selling education is this:

Free webinar → $495 weekend seminar → $5,000 intensive course → $20,000 master course

It's called upselling. You get lured in with something free, the content in that free resource convinces you that you should learn more from that person or company, so they sell you on the cheaper weekend course, and the information in that course convinces you that you should invest in the heftier courses. To move people through that funnel, gurus have to give sales pitches. That's just how the funnel works for the people or companies who make money from selling education.

When you know that's how the products are structured, you can better position yourself to get the most out of the money you invest. For example, I did one of those $495 Robert Kiyosaki Rich Dad seminars when I was first starting out. I knew to expect the sales pitches going in. I was fine with that; it's how they make their money. But I also knew that around those sales pitches would be legit real estate investing information. Sure enough, probably half of the weekend was sales pitches. The other half, however, provided pertinent information that I could, and did, use for my investing career.

Those small bits of information I learned about real estate investing, around all the sales pitches, ended up being critical for my investing journey. I don't think my investing journey would have been what it was without that information. Did I get $495 worth of information from that weekend? Abso-freaking-lutely.

That's how you have to look at any course or seminar that includes sales pitches. Sure, the sales pitches can be annoying, but screw them—focus on the information and get what you came there for. The information is there. You just have to pay attention.

When Should You Do a Guru Course?

The next thing to consider about a guru course is timing. *When* you take the course is critical.

The $495 weekend courses—no big deal. You can take those at any time, and it won't be a huge loss if you don't get anything out of it. But once you start getting into the $5,000 or $20,000 courses or the expensive coaching programs, you're at an actual risk for major financial loss if you can't use the information you get from the courses.

Bear with me on this one, as I'm going to get into completely unproven and unscientific theory here...

I'm a big believer in building things organically. For example, say I'm a brand new investor and I'm trying to figure out what I want to invest in. I get the brainiac idea to buy and run a hotel. On paper, I can absolutely figure out how to do this and try to make it happen. There's no doubt about that. But is owning a hotel something that comes naturally to me or is part of my life plan? I'm not questioning fate here or challenging your spiritual or religious beliefs, but how do I know a hotel is something that's supposed to happen in my life? Like I said, I can *make* it happen if I really push for it, but what if that entire venture is an uphill climb for me? Thinking back to analyzing my strengths (and interests) and following what comes naturally to me, how do I know owning a hotel is part of all that? I don't.

Maybe owning a hotel is 100% in my natural grain and is supposed to be in my life. Maybe it's something that comes very easily for me. But do I want to invest a ton of effort and capital right away into buying a hotel just to figure that out? No, I don't.

I'm more of a believer in baby steps. Rather than going straight for the hotel purchase, maybe I attend some hotel owner conferences. I do some research. I make connections. I see if this route begins to come naturally for me. If it does, great. Invest a little here, invest a little there, and keep building on that. That way, not only am I building my foundation in the hotel ownership business bit by bit in order to create a more solid footing for myself, but if at any point my path begins to change, I'm not losing everything I have in one fell swoop. I'm taking the time to ensure that buying that hotel comes naturally to me and is supposed to happen. Whereas, if I dump a ton of effort and money into it while just hoping or assuming it's what I'm supposed to be doing, I could end up losing it all if I find out this gig isn't for me.

If you're a brand new investor and you spend a little bit of time researching different investment strategies and you decide to just pick one of those strategies and dive in, that's totally cool. Just remember that you probably don't know what's really in your cards just yet. As I explained about my experience, rental properties just came naturally to me. But it took a little time and experience for me to figure that out.

Long before I figured out that rental properties were my thing, I was sitting in one of those $495 weekend courses. In that course, flipping sounded great. It sounded fun, it sounded lucrative, and it sounded like something that I could have the skill set for. At that moment, I could have signed up for a $5,000 or $20,000 flipping course.

It's a good thing I didn't! Had I gone to that expensive course, I probably would've learned a lot of good and legit information about flipping, but once I got out into the world to put it all to use, I'd have encountered all the reasons flipping isn't my thing. That $5,000 or $20,000 would've gone to waste.

Don't totally rule out the expensive courses. Just put in some effort beforehand making sure the strategy you are about to invest in is really the strategy for you. Don't take an expensive course with the intention of *buying* that strategy for yourself. Meaning, don't put money toward a strategy in order to make it come to you. Find the strategy first and *then* invest the money into it.

Here's another example. Imagine you got involved in a small flipping deal. Your rich uncle convinced you to flip a house with him, and you start to figure out you're actually pretty good at it. You're surprisingly handy with a hammer and managing contractors, you're unexpectedly able to put some creative financing solutions in place, and you find yourself really taking command of the project. Then once you flip it, you pocket a notable penny from it. You think to yourself, "Hey, I was pretty good at that. It came very naturally to me. All the while, I really didn't totally know what I was doing. I wonder what would happen if I were to learn more about everything I just did." That might be the right time to take the $5,000 course and see what you get from it. Does it help increase your profits on your next flip? If the answer is yes, you may really be onto something. Maybe you jump into the $20,000 flipping course then or invest in a flipping coach?

That is the organic approach to the expensive courses. Whereas most people read online about different investment strategies, decide one of those strategies is definitely the one for them, and then they fork over $20,000 because once they take that course, they'll know everything they need to know and their lives will be complete. See the difference?

Guru courses and seminars aren't bad. In fact, they can be extremely beneficial for a new investor. But you have to be careful about how you use them.

Here's a checklist to help you to ensure you get the most out of guru courses:

√ **Start small.** Start with less-expensive courses and build up to the more expensive courses slowly and with caution.

√ **Have reason to believe the course will help you.** If you have no reason to believe flipping is in your life's cards, don't drop a ton of money into flipping courses just yet. Have some kind of baseline evidence that suggests you have a future in the particular strategy you are about to invest a lot of money into.

√ **Work around the sales pitches.** There is valuable information before and after the sales pitches. Keep an ear out for it, look for it, and take it in. The sales pitches are bound to be there, so just plan to ignore them.

√ **Follow gurus you resonate with.** Hopefully long before you've bought into a course or seminar, you've read a book or two from the guru who is putting on the course or seminar. Make sure it's someone you resonate with. As I said, I've always resonated with Robert Kiyosaki's teachings, but never with Dave Ramsey's. If I were to invest $495 into a weekend-long Dave Ramsey seminar, it's not a major loss to my wallet if it doesn't pan out, but why would I do that in the first place knowing Dave Ramsey's entire outlook on finances is completely contradictory to my goals?

One last question I hear regarding the guru seminars is, "Why should I pay for information when there's so much free information available online?"

That's a fair question, but the answer is easy:

• **Diversification.** Diversification is always a good thing. Get some free advice, and get some paid advice. It's rare that trusting one source for anything in life is a safe way to go. Mix it up. You never know where the golden piece of advice is going to come from that sends you flying down your path to success.

- **Credibility**. One way to pick the dependable voice out from the crowd is to go with a guru with a loyal following or a public figure with a proven track record. At the point someone is putting on a guru course or seminar or has a book out, it's likely they have some kind of experience to back up what they are teaching. I've not heard of many 'gurus' who haven't actually done what they're being paid to teach. In the world of TMI and idiots, checking in with an actual guru on occasion can be really helpful.

- **Organization of information.** When I released my first eBook on turnkey rental properties years ago, a lot of people who were on the big real estate investing website that I wrote for asked, "Why would I pay $30 for an eBook when I can get all of the information right here online for free?" That's another easy answer. If you're piecemealing a bunch of information together, you can't know that you're getting all of the pieces, getting accurate pieces, and that you're putting the pieces together in the right way. The eBook I wrote saves readers a heck of a lot of time trying to find and put all the pieces together successfully. I'm also a known credible source for turnkey rental properties, so readers know they can trust the information I give them. Is a $30 investment[10] worth that to you? It would be for me, all day long. Why put in all that work to potentially get inaccurate information when I could spend a little bit of money and have it all handed to me on a silver platter?

---

10   The price of the eBook has since dropped from $30 since it's a few years old now. It's available on Amazon! *Turnkey Rental Properties 101: The Definitive Guide to Hands-Off Rental Properties.*

At the end of the day, it's about finding a balance. Invest what you need to in order to become successful, but don't dive deep into that investment without proper footing. Otherwise, you could lose before you ever earn anything. Accidentally spending your life savings has never helped anyone build confidence as an investor. I truly believe that if you're following the path laid out for you, the resources will present themselves in a way that doesn't break your bank or your wallet. At the same time, investing some of your own resources into education can help prove your intention and dedication, be it to yourself or to others, and that can be invaluable.

chapter fourteen

Choose Your Focus

We already talked about the beginning stages of narrowing your focus (remember the picture of the funnel?), but now we're going to move into actually choosing a focus.

One mistake I was making while I was in the exploration phase was not narrowing down my focus enough. While I did it right in the beginning—started wide and with no restrictions—I eventually caught myself staying too broad. I had followed the funnel concept, but I hadn't gotten narrow enough. I had narrowed down my general interests to things like passive income and leveraging, but I hadn't used those interests to pick a specific strategy to pursue. The only thing I had narrowed myself down to was knowing that if I wanted to get out of my corporate job, I was either going to have to start a business or do something in real estate investing. Those are infinitely broad focuses.

For the longest time I was pursuing both of those—business and real estate investing—studying everything I could about them. One day I woke up and realized it was no wonder I hadn't started gaining any traction—I was stuck because I was learning a little about a lot. For me to be able to actually get started with anything, I was going to have to shift into learning a lot about a little.

This is when I realized I needed to pick a strategy so I could make a plan and pursue it. This is more specific than the narrowing that happens in the exploration phase—this is actually choosing something to pursue.

Choosing your focus should be a combination of an approach that appeals to you and one that matches your goals. People so often dive into a real estate investment strategy because it's highly marketed or sounds appealing, yet they know nothing about how the strategy works or whether it would be a fit for them. If you don't yet know your goals at this point, you shouldn't choose a focus yet! Being clear on your goals, or at least having an idea of your goals, is imperative for choosing a strategy because so many different real estate investing strategies accomplish so many different goals. If you choose a focus or strategy that goes against your goals, not only will you be swimming upstream the whole time, but you will likely never succeed to the extent you could if you chose something more fitting. There is no wrong strategy and no wrong goal, so there is no reason not to be honest with yourself about what you hope to accomplish and what kind of investing you're interested in.

In no way do you have to stick with whatever strategy you choose for the rest of your life, but you've got to have a starting point. It's only when you can choose a specific strategy to pursue that you can begin to learn what you need to about it so that you can succeed with it. You may hear people in business world talking about 'picking a niche'—it's the same concept here. If you're all over the place and not niching it down, you aren't going to get very far.

Thinking about your *why* and acknowledging what things grabbed your attention during your exploration phase, go ahead and choose what strategy you want to pursue. You don't have to know everything about that strategy just yet, and you can always change strategies down the road if you get into it and realize maybe it isn't quite right for you, but you have to choose something to focus on.

Once you choose your focus or your strategy…

chapter fifteen

Study Up!

Things start to get a little more serious now. Serious in the sense of—while the work can still be fun and an enjoyable part of the journey, there's a slightly more studious level required now than when you were just playing in the playground of possibilities. Now you need to learn the ins and outs of the real estate investing strategy you've chosen.

Much like when you start into the exploration phase, the door leading into learning about a particular strategy may seem to lead into a total abyss of options for what to learn, with no real guidebook on where to start. But also just like with the exploration phase, you just have to walk through that door. Start looking around everywhere and begin collecting what information you can. As you collect more and more information, you'll be able to start sifting through it all and pulling what you need and organizing it.

What Information to Get

It may not be obvious initially what information you should be going after as you begin to learn about a strategy. As you continue to dive in, it will probably start to become a little more obvious about what things you need to know. But to help give you some guidance on the most critical things you should know for any investment strategy, here are the minimum things I think you should understand before moving forward with any investment:

- What factors make this strategy successful?
- What can cause this strategy to fail?
- How do you run the numbers?
- What are the primary risk factors?
- How can you specifically mitigate those risks?

If you can intelligently answer these questions about a strategy, you probably know enough to try out a deal. But really know the answers; don't just know rote answers that don't actually confirm an in-depth understanding.

Initially, start to learn the answers to these questions by explicitly looking for them throughout your studying. Study everything, but especially keep an eye out for those things. Learn how to run the numbers, learn the success factors and risk factors, and learn the risk mitigations unique to the strategy.

Once you feel like you've gotten a good basic education, apply this knowledge to an actual property. This isn't a property you're actually going to buy, but look for real-life properties that you could hypothetically invest in. You can look at websites like Zillow or Redfin, or you can have an agent send you a list of available properties. This will first give you practice in how to choose a property. If you can't figure out how to select a property from a list of options, then that's more education you need to go back and learn. Then, once you've chosen a [hypothetical] property, analyze it in such a way that supports those knowledge points you've just learned about it.

For example, ask yourself these questions about the property:

- What about this property specifically suggests to you that it will be a successful investment?
- What are the numbers?
- What are the risk factors?
- What risk mitigations are in place?

When people tell me they're considering investing in a particular property, quite often they can't tell me why that property might be a good investment. This means they don't actually know what they're doing. If an investor can tell me *specifically* why they believe a property will be a good investment and identify the risks and risk mitigations in place, it means they likely know enough to move forward and have a decent chance of success.

While the knowledge you need is fairly straightforward, you're likely not going to get it all at once. You're more likely to go through several rounds of: getting information, applying it to hypothetical properties, seeing where the gaps are in your education, going back to get more education, trying it out on more properties, and round and round. All while every time you think you've learned something, you read or learn something that seems to contradict it. It can take a while to learn it all! So don't let yourself get too frustrated; remind yourself that learning to be a real estate investor is a journey, not an event. Remember your *why* along the way and keep the learning process fun.

Where to Get the Information

One thing to keep in mind during this phase is the sources you're getting your information from. This is relevant to the exploration phase as well, but it's not as critical there. Since now you're collecting the knowledge that's ultimately going to move you into trying out a deal, you want to make sure as best you can that the information you're procuring is accurate. While the internet is hugely beneficial for limitless information, there are rarely checks and balances on what information is being offered. Someone could easily and freely pose as a successful property flipper, for example, and spout off gobs of information that is not only inaccurate, but if followed, could get you in a lot of trouble. It's critical to be able to know whether the information you're getting is accurate or not. But how can you tell? Here are some tips to consider when trying to decipher legit information from bad information:

- **Look for reputable sources.** You may not always be able to tell who's reputable and who's not, but start by thinking about some of the big guns of real estate investing: Robert Kiyosaki, Barbara Corcoran, Warren Buffett, or other well-known names. There's little question that those people know what they're doing and are worth listening to. They might not be overly helpful for detailed strategy specifics, but they're a good place to start. For less obvious sources, you can probably search someone's name on the internet and see what information is generally published about them and their reputation.

- **Listen to them talk.** There are few easier ways to get a feel for someone than by listening to them talk. Do they sound like they are trying to sell you something or do they sound like they're conveying genuine information? Are they coming at it from a cocky place or a more authentic place? Listening to someone talk is especially easy today with the advent of podcasts. You get to hear real conversations straight from the horses' mouths. Books and blogs are good too; you just don't always get the voice behind the words. Feeling someone out isn't really a measurable criterion and maybe not everyone has an intuitive sense about people, but you really can get a lot just from how people speak.

- **"Don't take advice from someone you wouldn't trade shoes with."** The mantra I use every single day, especially in real estate investing and business. If I want to be a flipper and someone who is extremely successful in flipping wants to give me advice, I should probably consider that advice. But if someone who spends all his or her time on online forums yammering on about what a great flipper they are, I should probably be hesitant to take that advice. Why would that successful of a flipper be spending all their time on online forums? Ask yourself, "Is this person successfully doing what it is I'm trying to learn?" If the answer is yes, great! If I'm not sure, I should pause before taking the information as gold. Or, more broadly than just the specific strategy, is that person advocating for the type of lifestyle you're wanting and the goals you're trying to achieve? If they live a different lifestyle than you're wanting or are achieving different goals, you should think twice before taking their advice.

- **Increase your knowledge base.** The more you know and the more education you have, the more you can get a sense for what things make sense, what might not make as much sense, and what ideas or concepts seem to line up with reality. When you know very little or have very little education, it's nearly impossible to distinguish information that might be completely false or off-base. But the more data points you have, so to speak, the more you can see trends or patterns that will help you better differentiate good information from bad.

As you get farther along with your studying, start thinking about putting a plan together. This plan can be similar to a business plan, but it doesn't have to be quite so formal. You need a plan that identifies what you're trying to accomplish, how you intend to accomplish it, and your measurements for success. Basically you want to make a plan for how you want to go forward and what things you're going to look for along the way.

For example, if you've chosen your strategy and done lots of studying and you want to do a deal tomorrow, what do you need to know? What are you looking for, what are you going to watch out for, and how are you going to decide what deal(s) to pursue? The answers to all of these questions will come from those knowledge areas mentioned earlier.

One last caution about the studying period: beware of analysis paralysis. Because real estate investing can be very intimidating and we may have a lot of money riding on our success, it's easy to think we don't know enough yet to actually pursue a deal. It's good to have that sense of caution so that you don't try something too soon, but there are a lot of aspiring real estate investors who never get into the industry because they remain paralyzed in the analysis and education phases. Real estate investing is very much an on-the-job training industry. There's no way to know everything you need to know before you get started. Of course the opposite end of that spectrum is jumping in too soon before you know enough, but if you can use the guideline of whether or not you can intelligently explain to someone why you're pursuing a particular deal, you can know if you're safe to jump in or not. If you can't explain why a particular deal seems promising, keep studying. If you can explain it and you actually understand what you're explaining, it's time to make a move.

Put your floaties on and plug your nose, because it's time to jump in.

chapter sixteen

Make a Move

You have to make a move eventually; otherwise you're just doing all of this to kill time and you'll never see a return. As I said, the biggest real estate investing lessons you will ever learn will come from experience. I always equate this part of the getting-started process to something I learned when I started flying airplanes. I was told once by a seasoned military and airline pilot that becoming a great pilot happens mostly through experience. The real training for a pilot comes from making mistakes in the air. The purpose of flight school is just to teach us enough to prevent the *big* mistakes. This is why most pilot jobs require a certain number of flight hours from applicants before they'll even be considered for the job; if every pilot could learn everything they needed to in flight school and didn't learn more in the air, flight hours wouldn't matter.

Real estate investing is exactly the same as flying in that regard. There's no way to never make a mistake as an investor. And it's by making those mistakes that you build experience. If you wait until you think you have enough education to prevent you from ever making a mistake, you're wasting time getting started as you'll never know enough *until* you get started.

Your first move as a real estate investor doesn't have to be a huge move. There's no reason to dive into a million-dollar multi-family apartment complex as your first investment. Even flipping properties can be a big undertaking for a brand new investor, and an expensive project if done incorrectly. There are plenty of investment opportunities that involve much lower risk and lower requirements for capital investment so you aren't having to put everything you have on the line to 'try something'. You can try just a portion of your available capital. You can also, if you have the opportunity, partner with someone experienced for a deal while you get your feet wet.

Oftentimes there will be nerves associated with getting started, which is completely understandable. This is the point where you can go back and reread the chapter about failure. You can't fail; you can only experience learning opportunities. But within that is the reminder of knowing that what you invest could be lost and why it's important to not go too big for your first deal. But assuming you're investing within appropriate levels, one way to help with your nerves is to ask yourself, *"What is truly the worst-case scenario?"* You might be surprised to realize that oftentimes the worst-case scenario isn't as bad as our minds like to concoct it to be. There's a part inside of most of us that perceives situations like this to be life or death. If we fail at something, it's as if our insides think our lives are being threatened so we go into a full-panic and assume the end is here.

When I was deciding whether or not to pursue my very first investment—the beach bungalow in Nicaragua—I got to the point where it was time to make a decision about whether to sign the contract or not. I had done all of my due diligence, I had gotten all of my questions answered, and all seemed to be in order. It was at this point my nerves started to kick in. I remember sitting back in my chair one day debating whether or not I was going to go for it. I asked myself, *"What is the worst-case scenario? What will truly happen if the whole thing tanks out?"* I sat there thinking about it, and I realized that in fact the true worst-case scenario wasn't that I was going to die or my life would be over or that I would be ruined for the rest of my life, which was what my mind and body were fairly convinced would be the case. The true worst-case scenario was that I lost the $30,000 I invested. That's it. In this case, I didn't even have a loan to worry about because the remaining 70% of the purchase price was being seller-financed. Literally, the worst thing that could happen was I lost $30,000.

While $30,000 is a lot of money, and for some people it may be an entire year's salary, it wasn't a death sentence. The realization that truly all that would happen is I lost a lot of money was mind-blowing. I was sure my life would've been on the line, because that's what my current level of nerves was suggesting. But that wasn't the case; my mind was playing a trick on me. If you've been human long enough, you're well aware that our minds can blow things out of proportion to fairly epic levels and for seemingly no good reason. Once you realize our minds are capable of that, you can better navigate different situations. Once I realized that truly the worst thing that could happen was I might lose money, and it was literally nothing more than that, I felt better moving forward. And you know what ended up happening? I lost that $30,000. In fact, that's not all I lost; I actually lost $40,000 after having invested another $10,000 in the same project because I ended up going down to visit the development several times and felt like it was a really good deal.

Guess what happened after I lost that $40,000? Nothing: I was still alive, my life hadn't changed, and the only way anyone would've even noticed my loss would be if they had known my previous bank balances and now saw them with a $40,000 lower balance. The only major thing that came out of that $40,000 loss was me having made amazing connections in the real estate world, which ended up being the connections that ultimately got me out of engineering and into my own real estate investing business. Looking back, that $40,000 almost seems like a small price to pay for everything I got out of it.

At the time I lost $40,000, I had a high-paid corporate job where I could afford to lose $40,000. Not to say it didn't hurt me or my bank accounts, but I was still able to support myself financially despite the loss. Not everyone can afford to lose $40,000. For those people, a prospective $40,000 loss as the worst-case scenario should deter them from that deal. If the worst-case scenario on a deal is enough to tank you, find a smaller deal to start with.

By analyzing the *true* worst-case scenario in an investment deal, you should quickly be able to either: eliminate your unjustified fear or realize you're diving in too deep. It's just that simple.

chapter seventeen

Learn and Continue

As already stated a million times, the best news about real estate investing (and about life in general) is that there's no real such thing as failure; there are only learning opportunities, if you choose to see them that way. There's no doubting that in the moment of 'failure' it may feel like an epic failure and potentially a sign of your worth as a person, but those are just feelings. It doesn't mean that what you feel is the truth really is the truth. It's fine to let those feelings fly while they're there, but then it's time to pick yourself back up and figure out what you've just learned and get back out there. It's only when you can do this that you can truly become successful.

When you hit a bump in the road, big or small, the easiest and most efficient path out of it may look something like this:

1. Assess what went wrong and why.
2. Decide how you can course correct to avoid that same problem in the future.
3. Come up with a new plan.
4. Pursue the new plan.
5. If (when) failure happens again, rinse and repeat.

Navigating failure can be just this simple. Your real estate investing journey becomes a rinse-and-repeat process. You try something, you learn from it, you try something again, you learn from it again. This will be your entire experience. Hopefully, each time you learn something and try something new, you're doing it better than you were before. Eventually, repeating this cycle will get you to your desired level of success.

As with anything, there's no wrong way to get into real estate investing or to be a real estate investor. There are just ways that lessen your chances of catastrophic 'learning opportunities' as well as ways to make the process more efficient and more focused on your goals. No matter how you do it, as long as you're willing to learn along the way, you will be in a position to do the best that you can do as an investor.

part five

Our Pain, Your Gain:
Real-Time Experiences
of Successful Investors

chapter eighteen

Learning From Others

Once you do start getting into the how-to guides for various real estate investment strategies, you might notice a lot of them only tell you how to do the strategy while not necessarily painting the whole picture of the strategy. Few how-to guides offer a rating system for the effort level, skill level, and frustration level that come with each of the strategies.

One of the best ways to better understand different real estate investing strategies is to hear about them directly from experienced investors who are already succeeding with them.

- What's the actual reality I can expect with this strategy?
- Is the strategy overly difficult?
- What skills will I really need?
- What are the risks with the strategy?
- How can I help mitigate those risks?
- Will I like this strategy?

As I said numerous times throughout the book, your investing isn't going to look 100% like someone else's investing (which is why the how-to guides by themselves don't usually work). The key really is in gathering as much information as you can about the different strategies, self-assessing where your skills, strengths, and interests are, and coming up with a plan based on those.

To help in gathering all of that information, I interviewed successful real estate investors who all do different strategies. The intention with these interviews is to help give you that real-life perspective on what some of these strategies look like once you really get into them. You still aren't going to have all the answers once you go through these, but you will have more information to help you assess what path you may want to think about pursuing.

While you never want to take advantage of the opportunity to connect with successful investors by demanding them help you or asking them to teach you everything they know for free, it can be very valuable to connect with people who have already paved their own path and can share their experiences. This is why I purposefully selected the investors that I did for these interviews—all of them currently mentor individuals in their selected strategies. Many of them have created their own training programs, some of them lead local real estate meetups, and most of them offer a lot of valuable resources online. At the end of each interview will be the investor's bio and links to be able to connect with them. Reach out to them if their strategy seems to resonate with you! That's what they're here for.

Before diving into the interviews, here's a quick reference guide to the types of real estate investing strategies that are addressed in the interviews:

Buy-and-Hold

This basically means rental properties. Buy-and-hold means exactly what it says—you're buying a property and then holding onto it versus selling it.

When you buy-and-hold a property, you're profiting through the hold. So if you buy a rental property and hold it for 30 years, you're hopefully profiting from appreciation over those 30 years as well as through monthly cash flow.

Some people buy a rental property and hold it forever, even passing it down through their family line through inheritance. For a lot of investors, the ability to pass on wealth to their family members is the reason they get into real estate investing in the first-place, so buying rental properties for long-term holding is perfect for this as the properties continue to get passed down through the family lines.

While most people think of rental properties as smaller residential properties, the term buy-and-hold could also be used for commercial properties. This could be a retail shopping center, which are basically commercial rental properties as businesses rent the spaces, or it could be a large apartment building. While a large apartment building is considered a commercial property and is run as a business, it's essentially offering rental properties to residential tenants who live in each of the individual units.

You could also technically buy-and-hold something like a piece of land. With land, you aren't necessarily renting that land to anyone or making money monthly on it, but you are holding the land for profit.

Buy-and-Rehab

Buy-and-rehab is a lot of what was talked about earlier when I compared traditional investing to turnkey investing. Buy-and-rehab is a value-add opportunity; you're buying a distressed property and then rehabbing it with the intention of forcing appreciation through that rehab. A more recent term for this strategy is called the "BRRRR model". BRRRR stands for *buy-rehab-rent-refinance-repeat.*

In the case of buy-and-rehab, the assumption is that you're holding the property even after the rehab is complete and the appreciation has been forced. At that point, after you've rehabbed the property, you've placed tenants in the property and are now collecting monthly cash flow. You then gain all of the benefits of holding a rental property, with the added bonus of that initial jump in equity through the rehab.

Flipping

What a lot of investors do after rehabbing a distressed property, instead of holding it, is to then sell it. Because you've just forced the appreciation on the property through the rehab, you can now sell it for more money than you put into it. The difference between what you put into it and what you sell it for is profit to you. Some cases when an investor may do this versus holding a property they've just rehabbed could be:

- to continually snowball funds from one property into another (whereas with holding the money remains tied up in the one property) as a means of profit
- because the property won't have positive monthly cash flow from tenants
- the investor isn't interested in having rental properties

Flipping is considered an active investment strategy versus a passive strategy, which is what rental properties are considered. Flipping is done over the short-term, not the long-term.

Wholesaling

Wholesaling is the most active of the strategies. While a wholesaler themselves may have set up systems and processes so that they themselves aren't constantly active, the work to wholesale in general is very active.

Wholesaling is like match-making for real estate investors. A wholesaler finds a property that an investor might be interested in, acquires the contract for a property and assigns that contract to the end-investor. The wholesaler makes money either from assigning a fee or by collecting the difference between what the property is sold for and what the end-investor purchases it for, or both.

Wholesaling is one of the most common real estate strategies advertised to new investors because you can do it with very little capital, and it's a great way to get your feet wet in terms of learning what investors look for, what properties make for good investments, and all the other wheelings and dealings of the real estate investment world. However, it's important to realize wholesaling is actually a job rather than an actual investment strategy.

Turnkey Rental Properties

You've already learned about turnkeys and the model they follow, but now I can explain it using slightly different terms.

Investing in turnkey rental properties is only a method of *buying* a rental property, not a method of *owning* a rental property. Once you buy a turnkey rental property, it's like owning any other rental property in terms of what is required to be successful with it and how to manage it.

Because a turnkey rental property is in fact a rental property, like any other rental property but without having to do any of the rehab or management work, it is a buy-and-hold investment. The person or company who sells you the turnkey rental property is essentially acting as a flipper. They go find and buy the distressed property, potentially from a wholesaler, they rehab it, and then they sell it to you for the new value of the property.

See how all of these strategies start to fit together?

A couple more terms to understand:

Landlord

If you own a rental property, or any kind of buy-and-hold property, somebody has to manage that property if you want it to continue functioning. This person is the landlord. As an investor, you may choose to be the landlord for your property yourself. In this case, you're responsible for finding and screening tenants, managing the tenants, handling contracts, managing repairs to the property, and in some cases, managing the eviction process.

Ultimately, it's up to you as the landlord to maintain the property and the returns on the property.

Property Manager

The alternative to you being the landlord on your own property is to hire a property manager to do it for you. This may be an individual person or a property management company. You pay a small fee—usually a percentage of the monthly rent—to the manager or the management company and they do all of the aforementioned tasks on your behalf.

Now that you have a basic understanding of the most fundamental real estate investing strategies, now you can hear straight from the mouths of professional (and successful) investors who have mastered those strategies.

chapter nineteen

Moneeka Sawyer

Primary strategy: Buy & Hold–Landlord
Location: San Jose, CA
Location of investments: San Jose, CA
25 years' experience

Q: Can you describe your investment strategy?

A: I call my strategy Blissful Buy and Holds. It's a buy and hold strategy based on keeping it fun, low-stress, and low effort. I also focus on making sure I don't have to spend much time managing my business.

I buy rental properties local to where I live in San Jose. I live in a very high priced area so it's hard to even break-even on a property for a few years after I buy it. So I invest mostly for appreciation and enjoy the cash flow I get after a few years of ownership as a bonus.

I don't want to pay for property management, which is why I manage my properties myself. But I don't want all the headaches often associated with being a landlord. In order to keep myself blissful I have developed scripts and processes to check-out and train my tenants. Real estate is a people business, and the single biggest factor in whether my rental property business is blissful is going to be in how I handle my relationships.

The first thing I do is I buy properties in areas that the kinds of tenants I would like to have want to live in. Then, when I'm considering someone as a tenant, I make sure I call their references. (I never skip this step!) Then I have a conversation with them to set expectations that they will be managing the house as if it is their own. I won't be dealing with toilets, lightbulbs, etc. They will be, and thus they won't have to wait for my schedule. If they like this idea, we move forward to the next conversation. If not, I move to the next prospect.

For me, finding a tenant is a bit like dating. We take it one step at a time until we decide we want to work together. Ultimately, the tenants are the key to my success; hence my strong focus on them more than anything else.

The other important factor as part of my processes that allow me to be a fairly hands-off landlord is with repairs and rehabbing. For both of those, I don't do any fixes myself. I always work with contractors or handymen for "the big fixes." I spend the time to meet with contractors before I hire them on to do a job for me. Also, I always check some references on them. Again, it's all about the people. Once I hire them, I do random visits while they are doing the job to make sure we are meeting our time and budget targets and to help them if they have any questions. I don't stand around and chat. Be careful, because it seems contractors love to chat with the homeowner, and they'll charge you for their time! Be friendly, but professional. Nurture the relationship and they will take really good care of you.

I've outlined all of my processes in a home study course I created, which you can find in my author bio.

Q: How much time do you typically spend on your investments?

A: Most months I spend no time on my investments. But if a transition happens [when I'm between tenants] or I need to do a big fix, I may spend 20–30 hours in a month. It averages out to about 5–10 hours a month.

Q: Can you walk us through a typical deal?

A: My typical process is:

1. *Search for a property.* I have a realtor who is constantly sending me properties based on specific search criteria I have identified. So I'm always looking for property. I might spend a couple hours every couple weeks looking at properties. There are times when I'm aggressively searching and then I spend more time. Maybe five hours a week on the search.

2. *Write offers.* It takes me about an hour to review and sign an offer. I often will write about 10–15 offers before I close a property.

3. *Order and review inspections and other docs.* I only do this once I'm in contract and it takes about 1–3 hours.

4. *Sign closing docs*: takes about an hour.

5. *Rehab*: I usually only need to do light rehabs. It usually takes my contractor 1–3 weeks. I spend about 1 hour a day on this.

6. *Finding tenants.* This is the labor intensive part for me. I probably spend about 20 hours to find the right tenant, and it takes 2–3 weeks.

7. *Move tenants in.* I welcome them to their new home— takes me about an hour.

8. *Ongoing.* After that I may only spend time on the property if something comes up and most things only require about an hour or 2 of my time, if I need to get involved at all.

9. *Turnovers.* If I have a turnover, this takes time for cleaning the property, fixing it up, and getting new tenants. I usually have turnovers about every five years.

Q: What skills do you use regularly for your strategy?

A: *#1–Running the numbers*

It's important to be able to figure out if a deal will be profitable, so I need to be able to interpret the numbers of a deal.

Nothing can happen in real estate unless the numbers work. I believe real estate is a people business when you are running the business. But you can't start the business if the numbers don't work. So, know how to run the numbers or you could end up in situations that could completely destroy your business.

#2–People skills

In the buy and hold business, people skills are crucial. I have to motivate my vendors, interview tenants, and manage my tenants in a way that keeps everyone happy. Also, I have to keep a great relationship with my real estate agent and my lenders.

Once you know a deal can work financially, you have to bring it into the fold of your business. This is where people skills are important. Without them, you will find that everything is harder. People will fight you and make your life harder than it needs to be. But if you have people skills, they will go out of their way to make your life easier. But don't worry, you don't have to be a social person, or super friendly. When I'm talking about people skills, I'm simply talking about treating people with basic kindness and respect.

#3–Curiosity

I have to be curious about houses and areas. This helps me to learn what I need to learn about a house before I buy it.

This is an interesting skill. It allows us to approach all challenges that come up as a puzzle rather than a cause for stress and upset. I have to say it is a key to bliss for me. I know a lot of landlords who don't have this skill, and they are often stressed out, angry, and bitter. Many of them end up leaving the rental business all-together. So I think developing a healthy dose of curiosity is very important to creating a long-term business.

#4–Problem solving, creativity, playfulness

Problems come up in any business and real estate is no different. I need to be able to look at any problem or challenge as a game so I can come up with several solutions and then pick the very best one. Sometimes the best one is a very creative solution others may not have thought of.

Playfulness goes along with curiosity. It allows you to approach issues that come up as a puzzle or a game. It keeps things light and allows the brain to function at its best. The brain shuts down when it is under stress. But it's more creative and resourceful when it's in a state of playfulness. Also, a state of playfulness is a better state to learn in. So, as your business is growing, being in a state of playfulness and curiosity will allow you to grow much more quickly, learn about markets more easily, and run the business with more flow, joy, and profit.

#5–Project management

Buying a house, fixing it up, and getting tenants is a project that needs to be managed from beginning to end. It takes systems, organization, confidence, and flexibility. Then whenever anything needs to be fixed in a house it's also a project that needs to be managed from beginning to end. The ability to see the big picture, as well as all the steps to achieve it, is very important. And then knowing how to implement the steps to achieve your desired results must be handled with care, focus, and grace.

Q: What are the primary risk points with your strategy? How severe is each risk point, and what are the consequences of each?

A: *Risk Point #1–Bad tenants*

Finding and keeping a good tenant. I think patience can mitigate this risk. People often rent too quickly out of fear. If you are able to wait for the right tenant, you will have much fewer tenant problems than if you rush to rent your place to the first okay applicant.

If you do get a bad tenant, the worst consequences are that you have to evict them, they damage the property so you have to get it fixed, and they can be a monthly headache with not paying rent, damaging the property, or demanding your attention to the property frequently.

Risk Point #2–Damage to the property

This happens, even to our own homes. Things happen. Get good tenants, and this will happen less frequently.

If substantial damage happens, the worst consequence is that you need to fix it and it eats up savings or all the cash flow you've made from a property for a while.

Risk Point #3–Property value drops

The real estate market is cyclical and at times home values drop. Do your homework on the areas you buy in. If you buy in an area where there are jobs and is generally safe, your property will most likely recover. But you have to be able to hold the property long enough for it to recover. Buy and hold is better as a long-term strategy because then you have more time to ride the cycles of the market and get the most benefits from it. Also, often even if property values drop, rents continue to go up. So, as long as you are okay with holding the property, and rents are covering your costs, you will be fine.

The worst consequence is the market drops and you need to sell the property, so you take a loss. Again, giving yourself time to ride out a down cycle will help to ensure you won't have to take a loss.

Risk Point #4–Expensive maintenance projects

This again will happen in every house, even the one you live in. Keep a reserve for these occurrences, so when something comes up you have money in the bank to handle them.

The worst consequence of this is if you don't have the funds in your reserve, you will have to defer the maintenance, or pull money out of your savings to pay for a project. This isn't the end of the world, but it can be very irritating. So protect yourself by keeping a reserve fund for your properties.

Q: What is your favorite part about your strategy?

A: I love how easy it is. It's easy because I have systems set up specifically with the intention of keeping things easy and in flow. That's my goal. I love project management (rehabbing) and dealing with tenants. I also love providing beautiful homes to people that love living there. And of course, I love how easy it is to get rich with real estate.

Everyone is going to have things they enjoy most in this business. Focus on doing the things you enjoy and hire out the rest. Many other landlords focus more on the money, on appreciation, or other factors. Of course I invest for those reasons, but my processes are set up specifically to keep things very easy for me. We reap what we focus on most.

Q: Is how you do your strategy now different in any way than it was when you started? If so, how is it different?

A: Absolutely! When I started I did everything like I was only going to do it once. It was time and energy intensive. I did everything manually every time.

For example, in the beginning every interview with a possible tenant was different. I would fill in the application with them and I would ask for different things with each application. Now the application process is its own system that I don't need to think about or spend any energy on. In the beginning I also dealt with issues as they came up, rather than setting expectations up-front with my tenants on how we would deal with issues that happened. My new system of dealing with issues is much less stressful.

Now I have most of what I do systematized. With the example of interviewing tenants, now I have a script that I use when having the initial conversation with a tenant about renting the house. After I get their application and do my due diligence on them, I go through a simple, clear process that determines if they are a good fit for my property or not. It keeps things running really smoothly. As far as dealing with issues and the tenants as things come up, now I have processes, contracts, emails, phone numbers all at my fingertips so I don't have to re-invent the wheel every single time I do anything. Things are much easier and quicker to handle now. I can take care of most things with a phone call or texts.

I definitely started doing everything the hard way and determined I didn't want to keep doing things that way. So along the way, I kept searching for ways to make things easier. And then when I found something that worked, I create a system around it. I'd write notes about it and keep the notes in a landlording folder on my computer so I always know where to find them. It took about 10 years for me to develop all of the systems I use now. Or at least I had most of them put together in the ~10 years, but I'm constantly improving and adjusting them. So they do evolve based on what I learn with each new property. There has been a lot of trial-and-error in developing my systems and even now I continue to find easier ways to do things, and then I improve the system.

Q: What advice would you give new investors starting out in this strategy?

A: Get started! This strategy is the most intuitive and easiest strategy out there. People have been doing this since the beginning of time, and everyone needs a place to live. So, do some research and buy your first property. You'll be glad you did.

Some tips for mitigating the risk points I mentioned:

Risk Point #1—Bad tenants

Vet your tenants well. Don't get impatient when finding a tenant. If you do your homework upfront, most tenant issues won't come up. However, if they do, follow the law and get them out so you can get new ones. In the end though, sometimes this is a stress point. Learn the skills to manage your own stress, so you can more easily manage difficult tenant relationships.

Risk Point #2—Damage to the property

This goes along with the answer above. The tenants you choose will determine how much damage there is to the property. However, damage always happens. Keep a reserve fund to deal with the upkeep and maintenance of the property. Also, when calculating how much rent you should charge, calculate in 5–10% of the rent for maintenance costs.

Risk Point #3—Property value drops

The real estate market is cyclical, so property values do drop periodically. Consider your real estate investing as a long-term endeavor. That way if the market values drop, you have time for them to recover. Give yourself enough time to be right about your investment.

Risk Point #4—Expensive maintenance projects

All houses need upkeep. Put major repairs in the budget so you have already saved for them when they come up.

With that said, focus on things going well. Don't get caught up in all the things that can go wrong. Prepare for them and mitigate them when you can, but when things do go wrong, don't freak out. Take a few deep breaths and change your attitude from frustration to curiosity to handle the issues.

Remember you reap what you focus on. Know your numbers, but run your business as a people business. Focus on creating strong relationships and keeping things positive for everyone, especially you.

Investor Bio: Moneeka Sawyer

Moneeka is the best-selling author of the book *Your Amazing Itty Bitty Blissful Real Estate Investing Book* and is the host of the Podcast Real Estate Investing for Women. Her expertise, and bliss-filled laugh, have been featured at the Nasdaq Marketplace, Harvard Club of Boston, Carnegie Hall, and on radio, podcasts and TV stations including ABC, CBS, FOX, and the CW impacting over 150 million people.

Moneeka is often described as one of the most blissful people you will ever meet. She has been investing in real estate for over 25 years, so has been through all the different cycles of the market. Still, she has turned $10,000 into over $2,000,000, working only 5–10 hours per month with very little stress.

While building her multi-million dollar business, she has travelled to over 55 countries, dances every single day, and spends lots of time with her husband of over 20 years and her adorable little puppy (who is the love of her life, but shhhh...don't tell her husband).

Moneeka loves teaching others how to build wealth like she has so they can create the life of their dreams. She's helped parents pay for their children's college educations and weddings. She's helped countless people to retire with the lifestyle they dreamed of. She's helped many people become millionaires. And they've all done this Moneeka's blissful way.

You can find her at:
www.Blissfulinvestor.com
www.RealEstateInvestingForWomenPodcast.com
www.RealEstateInvestingForWomenExtra.com

For social media links and access to Moneeka's best-selling book *Your Amazing Itty Bitty Blissful Real Estate Investing Book* and her home study course *The Blissful Real Estate Investor Formula* that outlines her exact investing strategies and processes, click on Moneeka's picture on the *NOT Your How-To Guide to Real Estate Investing* resources site www.aliboone.com/book-goodies.

chapter twenty

Jeb Brilliant

Primary strategy: Buy & Rehab
Location: Long Beach, CA
Location of investments: Indianapolis, IN
5 years' experience

Q: Can you describe your investment strategy?

A: At the moment my strategy is to BRRRR houses and apartments, which means I buy them distressed and at a discounted price, I rehab them, and then I either hold it for my own personal portfolio and rent it out or I sell it. I learned many years ago not to pigeon hole myself. When I bought a house to BRRRR but had the opportunity to sell it for a 50% return in almost no time at all with zero risk, I didn't say no because I only wanted to rent it, I pivoted and changed my strategy (so I sold it instead, which makes me technically a flipper as well as buy-and-rehab).

Q: How much time do you typically spend on your investments?

A: I do it full time, but that's about 40 hours/week. Though I'm able to take time off any time I want.

Q: Can you walk us through a typical deal?

A: Generally my process goes something like:

1. *Begin search for property.* Requires searching through wholesalers. I pretty much only buy from one whole-

saler because we have a long history and he takes care of me. It takes little time to look over a bunch of properties but running the numbers and doing background/due diligence on it can take hours. Over time things have changed with my methods as well as the industry. In this day and age you only have a few hours to a day or so to make a move on a property. Most wholesalers send out their best deals to several of their investors and leave it to the first to send in their earnest money. So you have to be quick.

2. *Negotiate for property.* Requires back and forth communication with seller. Because I'm buying from a wholesaler and he's a friend, I try not to negotiate unless the numbers are too close. Then we probably only go back and forth once and I like to do it over the phone versus with text. If negotiation can't be met, back to searching for properties. But for most investors, you would need to negotiate if they need to or can. It's important to try to get the BEST possible price without annoying your team or people.

3. *Close on property.* I ALWAYS do inspections and line up money, which means it's important to know where the money is coming from. I have a hard-money lender I like to use when necessary, or maybe for others it's a HELOC or it could just be cash sitting in a bank account. Requires complete due diligence to be done on property, which includes a property inspection! In my opinion it's SUPER important to do an inspection in nearly all cases. The ONLY deal I've ever lost money on is the one I didn't follow my checklist and forgot to do an inspection. ALWAYS DO AN INSPECTION!

4. *Begin rehab.* I like to keep rehabs short and quick but sometimes longer ones make you more money. I don't physically swing the hammer, I hire a general contractor (GC) who oversees the contractors. To keep things on track, I keep in touch with my GC and get weekly updates.

5. *Finish investment.* I hold the properties long term, but I usually refinance then hold. Meaning I will refinance the property and pull the money I poured into the property out so I can do it all over again. I always hire a property manager to find tenants for the property, and they continue to manage the property throughout my ownership.

Q: What skills do you use regularly for your strategy?

A: *#1–Subliminal people skills*

The biggest skill is dealing with people and their nuances. Remembering that general contractors are not always tech-savvy. Allowing people to think I don't know when they're lying to me. For example, I know one guy forgot to call me back, or was just putting it off, but he told me he broke his phone and lost all his text messages. Could be the case, and I let him believe that I believe him.

People like to think they are in control (I won't get into the way people process situations). If they think I believe them, they are likely to keep talking and not clam up. For me communication is one of the most important things. I try to weed out the lies and if they talk long enough they usually get around to the truth in some form or another.

I also get to know people and really listen to them, even if it's them bitching about their kids, spouses, etc. I let them know I'm a working stiff just like them. I do this so we become friends, and I feel like it makes it a little harder for them to want to screw me versus the next asshole investor.

#2–Thinking patiently

One of my mentors saw me react to a situation, and I was about to chew somebody out until he stopped me and told me to slow down and think patiently. This mentor is foreign and at first I thought he mixed some words up, but even if he did he was right. I needed to slow down and process before I acted instead of reacted.

The reason it's important to slow down is because I'm going to make better choices that are better thought out. For example, I've fired property managers before out of shear reaction, versus a thought out decision, and I've regretted it ever since.

#3–Micromanaging

Micromanaging, or specifically the lack of, is absolutely a skill to perfect. I tend to micromanage and my GCs hate it, so I started asking them for weekly updates and pictures. I still manage what's going on, but I try to let them make the mundane decisions though I've already usually told them what I want, which answers all the questions that come up during a rehab.

It is arduous, but I like to spend a lot of time talking to them about my vision of what a project should look like when it's done. I also hire GC's who invest so I can tell them I want a house done to a standard that will rent for $1,200/month, and we discuss what that is so they can make a decision on crown molding or not by themselves. Though we already had this conversation, so they know what my answer is going to be.

#4–Problem solving

This is probably the single most important skill to have. Pretty much every conversation is about a problem, and it's on the investors shoulders to lead your team to a solution. If it involves another person, I try to put myself in their shoes and understand their side of the situation. If it's a problem with a property then I consider all the options before making a decision. This is NOT easy, but it is necessary to run a business.

#5–Ability to put out fires

Putting out fires is really just problem-solving, and as a business owner this is what we do on a regular basis. We need to know how to "think patiently" and get through solving problems. A check I sent to my GC overnight hasn't arrived 3 days later, so I'm having to wire the money to him and eat the $30 fee. These are typical fires you have to put out.

#6–Managing managers

This is key because I'm not the GC, but I treat my GC as a manager and I have to make sure he's always on task.

7–Asset management

You are your own greatest advocate and so you need to manage your assets. I check on pricing all the time. If I'm told new standard duel hung double pained windows are $600 each and I need LOTS of them, I double-check (especially on these big expenses) because come to find out they really should only be $300 each installed. A good asset manager tries to always preserve capital.

 # 8—Networking

I'm always networking to grow my business in terms of always looking for more deals, better lenders, potential partners or investors. As much as I may be an antisocial grumpy curmudgeon sometimes, you just have to suck it up and fake it. Go out, shake hands with a smile on your face and pretend you are happy to be there.

Q: What are the primary risk points with your strategy? How severe is each risk point, and what are the consequences of each?

A: *Risk Point #1—The market drops*

This is a risk if you don't buy smart. If you purchased a house worth $100,000 for $50,000 and the market drops my 10% (which is a LOT), then I say you're still okay owning a house worth $90,000 that you paid $50,000 for. But if you purchased that $100,000 house for market value and it drops 10%, now you're upside-down on it and in a less desirable position. If you hold it for 10 years, though, you might be okay because in theory it should go up in value.

Risk Point #2—Unforeseen renovations

These will ruin an investment. I've had to sell a duplex because of this. An unforeseen $5,000 expense can wipe out $200/month in income for two years. This is all too common. You need to fix as much as you can when you do your rehab versus waiting for something to break. This will help your bottom line in the long run.

Make sure to have a contingency line in your budget for these unforeseen costs!

Q: What is your favorite part about your strategy?

A: The mail box money—not doing any work and someone sending me a check once a month (once the initial project/work is complete). I get checks for houses I'm not actively working on, though I'm working on other deals. Hopefully in a few more years I'll be able to lay back and relax and not have to work on this daily. Though I can easily take a few days off any time I want.

Also that I was able to close on a house from the beach once. I got a call that the house was mine if I signed the documents so I Docusign-ed them from my phone on the sand.

Q: Is how you do your strategy now different in any way than it was when you started? If so, how is it different?

A: Things are much easier now than they were when I started, just from having gained the experience that I have. While things are easier, my decision making is much more complex, though. A lot of what has changed is what properties I consider to be good deals or not. There are so few actual good deals out there and tons of mediocre deals. Being able to differentiate between the two has only come with experience.

I'm also trying to micromanage less than I used to. GC's hate that, and I don't want to piss them off because then they won't want to go work on my house and deal with me. So a lot of my evolution as an investor has been with the people relationships.

Q: What advice would you give new investors starting out in this strategy?

A: I think these are the most important things a new investor needs to know:

1. *Do your due diligence (DD).* Don't trust anybody who has a vested interest in you buying that property. They might say anything to get your business.

2. *Research and then JUMP in with both feet.* Analysis paralysis is probably the worst thing for an investor. If you get it you might never get started.

3. *Also wholesaling is NOT investing, it's a business unto itself.* Wholesaling is great and I love buying from wholesalers, but that's its own business. If that's all you do, you will have a business just like having any other business. It's not investing in real estate, its reselling real estate.

Also, people forget all too often that owning a rental home IS NOT PASSIVE. Besides staying on top of every aspect of the rehab and making sure things are getting done on time and up to my standards, I also have to make sure the contractors are not overpaying. I have to know how much everything costs or I'll get taken advantage of. Most property managers tell you that you need new windows, so they get you a price of $11k. $500/window. Well that doesn't work for me because windows are $300–$350 installed. So what do I do, spend a day on the phone lining up window companies, talking to my GC and getting prices. How much do I end up paying? $300/window, not $500. I save $4,400. That's a huge savings and time well spent, especially when I only make $4,800 or so per year net on the house. This is part of rehabbing and managing improvements—you can't slack on how things are done and how much they cost. If you do, you'll lose a fortune on your investments.

When I talk to people who work 70 hours/week and they want to supplement their income by investing in a BRRRR house, I tell them they're crazy. They need to find someone to partner with or a way more passive investment. Turnkeys, hedge funds, syndications, or something else, but NOT a single rental property that they do the work on themselves.

Investor Bio: Jeb Brilliant

Jeb Brilliant is a California-based real estate investor. He is currently focused on his dream of building a sizable investment portfolio. He has successfully BRRRR'd several properties, invested in apartment buildings, flipped houses, wholesaled, done hard money lending and note investing. He also mentors new investors and runs several local real estate meet-ups.

Jeb has a history in public relations (PR), is a long-time blogger, media relations specialist and is an expert in residence at the University of Southern California. He has counseled international telecom companies and currently holds multiple board positions in his local community. Jeb and his wife of 15 years live in Long Beach, California with their 2 children.

You can find him at:

www.PacificPropertyCollection.com

For social media links and access to Jeb's direct contact information, click on Jeb's picture on the *NOT Your How-To Guide to Real Estate Investing* resources site www.aliboone.com/book-goodies.

chapter twenty-one

Matt & Liz Faircloth

Primary strategy: Flipping & Multifamily Investing
Location: Trenton, NJ / New Hope, PA
Location of investments: New Jersey, Philadelphia
15 years' experience

Q: Can you describe your investment strategy?

A: Our strategy is primarily based around flipping, but in addition to the flipping we also do buy-and-rehab on large value-add multifamily properties. Both of these strategies involve buying properties that are in need of re-positioning and renovation. "Re-positioning" is adding value to buildings (improving the condition of the interior and/or exterior of the building). When we renovate residential buildings, it's to increase the value of the property, which is dictated by the market. Our other focus is on large value-add multifamily properties—we acquire apartment building complexes throughout the east coast. Because these are considered commercial buildings, the value of the building is dictated by the income the property receives, which is different from residential properties where the value is dictated by the market. So in these cases, our goal is to renovate the building in such a way that higher rents can be demanded, thus increasing the total income, which ultimately raises the value of the property.

Over the years, we've learned that we can't be good at everything (and we don't even want to be!) We have never been active "hands-on" flippers. This works for some fix and flippers, but it never

195

worked for us. We see ourselves primarily performing the project management task. Every day we ask: "What can I do today to advance this project?" Sometimes the answer is we need to meet with the contractor to ensure they are on timeline, sometimes it means we meet with our partner to discuss any bottlenecks, sometimes it means we need to communicate to our private lender about the project to keep him/her updated, or it may mean we meet with the realtor to discuss a marketing plan. Whatever it is, our primary "task" is keeping the project moving along and getting to the finish line.

Q: How much time do you typically spend on your investments?

A: For the smaller flips, we currently work on those 5–10 hours/week. Over time we developed partners and team members to help us manage the weekly flipping tasks, so that is the only reason it's more part-time. The larger buildings, the ones we are buy-and-rehabbing, equate to that of a full-time job.

Q: Can you walk us through a typical deal?

A: Sure!

1. *Choose the market or markets to focus on based on your criteria.* Requires analyzing various markets based on crime statistics, review of comparable sales, school system ratings, etc. Time requirement depends on the investor's pre-existing knowledge of the market.

2. *Begin to search for property in selected markets.* You need to begin to build a team in that area to source deals for you. You want to research the most active realtors who are selling the type of properties you want to flip. You also can find the most active wholesalers in these areas as well. You can also consider doing direct mail (and

many other marketing strategies) to find deals yourself. Time requirement to build these relationships could be 10 hours (initial contact phase with a handful of people). Then you need to invest two hours a week to maintain relationships which means analyze deals they send you, etc.

3. *Find deals that meet your buying criteria.* You need to confirm after repair value, walk the property with your contractor to determine the construction budget, use a good deal calculator to analyze the numbers, make an offer based on your profit goals, and negotiate with seller, find a win-win, and put under contract or walk away. Process can take up to 10 hours per deal.

4. *Due diligence and prepare for closing.* Due diligence consists of confirming construction costs, home inspection if that is part of your plan, set up insurance, confirm that title of property is clean, and set up financing with bank and/or private lender. Time required typically takes 1–2 months.

5. *Post closing.* Begin renovation process with contractor/ contractors hired. This should include a written and detailed scope of work, timeline and payment plan. Manage construction process and hold contractors to timeline and scope of work. Make timely payments to contractors at mutually agreed upon milestones. Property should be inspected on a regular basis. Time required could be anywhere from a few weeks to 6 months (this depends on the complexity of renovation and budget).

6. *Market for Sale.* This process should begin before construction is complete. It is important to hire a real-

tor who has a very strong track record of active and soldiers listings in your target market. Perform market research to price competitively. List the property and perform other creative marketing strategies to sell property. Choose the buyer that has the best offer and terms. Time required 2–4 weeks. If you are not under contract within this timeframe your property is most likely over-priced.

7. *Close sale with buyer.* Work with buyer to give access to property to perform appraisal and home inspection. Negotiate any credits or repairs based on the results of the appraisal and home inspection. Manage the process to keep closing on timeline. Close and go out to a nice dinner to celebrate! Time required 45–60 days.

Q: What skills do you use regularly for your strategy?

A: *#1—Ability to be analytical*

There are two aspects of being analytical. One is using your analytical skills to choose the right market and the second is being analytical to choose the right property to flip.

One place analytical skills are required is in choosing the right market. Some important aspects to consider when analyzing markets to flip in are:

- crime statistics
- school ranking
- job diversity
- employment opportunities

It's also important to analyze the neighborhood's real estate activity, such as:

- comparable properties for sale that have sold in the last six months

- how many homes (like the type you are looking to flip) are on the market

- how long these properties have been on the market (days on market)

You always want to be in a market that has low inventory and the days on market for the comps are less than 30 days.

Another place analytical skills are required is in then choosing the right property to flip. As you analyze a property to assess if it could be a good deal or not, you need to look at the property details, such as:

- the after repair value (ARV), based on comps

- costs to renovate

- holding costs, including realtor fees, utilities, insurance, property taxes, interest on loans (private money or conventional), HOA fees if applicable

- financing costs

Most newbies forget to account for unforeseen contingences in their financial analysis, as well as forgetting to account for holding costs such as taxes, water, and sewer.

#2–Negotiation

The next skill that is critical to have in this business of fixing and flipping property is negotiation. You are always negotiating, whether it's with buyers, sellers, contractors, a realtor, wholesaler, etc. When flipping, strong negotiation begins with finding and securing a deal to flip. Therefore you are working with homeowners or wholesalers. You need to know your numbers (costs and ARV) so you don't over pay for the property. Negotiating with a seller who is motivated makes it much easier. You have to give them what they want which is typically a quick sale and for that you get a discount.

You are also negotiating with the contractors. With contractors, they typically want more up front and no responsibilities for unforeseen issues. You have to make sure you have a fair payment plan in writing, clear and agreed upon in writing scope of work.

There are so many books on negotiation. If you aren't comfortable with negotiation or don't see yourself as a good negotiator, we would highly recommend "Never Split the Difference" by Chris Voss or "The Book on Negotiating Real Estate" by J Scott. Negotiation is all about finding the win-win in a situation.

#3–Construction knowledge and skills

It goes without saying that you do need some construction knowledge/skills to be effective at fixing and flipping houses. Now, you don't need to have 30 years' of experience in contracting by any means, but you should know the basics so that you can know what is "good" work and "bad" work when you do your walkthroughs with your contractors. In addition to just being able to distinguish between good and bad workmanship, you will also want to educate yourself on things like:

- local codes
- how to write a scope of work
- the importance of putting everything in writing
- establishing a payment plan with your contractor

You want to know enough so you don't get taken advantage of by your contractors, and your contractors are never ahead of you in payments, meaning that the value of the work that they have done is consistent with the amount of money they have been paid.

#4—Marketing and selling skills

You (or someone on your team) needs to have strong marketing and selling skills. You want to make EVERYONE aware of your product (the house you will fix and flip). It is so important and helpful to become friendly with the neighbors in the community you are flipping in and inform them of the work you are doing, and once you are ready, you should invite them to your open house. You want to make the neighbors your friends not enemies. And who knows, they might want to sell their house as well to you! It's also important to work with a realtor who sells a lot in your target market and who knows the type of buyers you are looking for. The most important aspect of being effective in marketing is *knowing your buyer/customer* first and then *anticipating their needs*.

#5—Financial management

You need to be organized and effective at managing the finances. You need to be constantly aware of all the money coming in and all the money going out. I know it's an obvious tip, but it's important to have a separate bank account for your flip projects. It is not only critical to manage your finances in an organized manner, but it's also important to pay your vendors on time, especially your contractors. While you don't want them to be ahead of you, you certainly want to pay them on-time so they keep working hard for you and showing up to do what you hired them to do.

#6—Problem solving

We hate to break the bad news here, but flip projects are not always going to go as planned. They rarely do! Once your contractor begins work, they can discover unexpected termite damage, for example. You might need to deal with difficult buyers or difficult sellers. Or you might discover at the end of the rehab the gas line can't be turned on because it needs to be replaced by a 3rd party utility company. All of these situations (and much more) have happened to us. These challenges can bring on delays to timeline and cost you more. The key skill here is solving the problem as quickly as possible and keeping the project on timeline as best as you can.

 # 7–Project management

Probably the most important skill in running fix and flip projects is project management. Bottom line—this is managing timeline, budget, and the team. This also includes anticipating bottlenecks and moving through challenges quickly. There is a huge coordinating skill in flipping homes, such as when to order and install cabinets, countertop, flooring, etc. Some of these materials can take longer than others to order and arrive, so strong project management skills are critical so that the project can stay on timeline and not be delayed. Part of project management is also coordinating with sub-contractor's schedules and keeping everything moving forward!

Q: What are the primary risk points with your strategy? How severe is each risk point, and what are the consequences of each?

A: *Risk Point #1–The market drops*

The market can change while you're renovating the property. This means that while you are renovating your flip, the local and global real estate market can shift—up or down for various reasons such as interest rates changing.

On the positive, sometimes this can work in your favor, where the market goes up while renovating. This has happened in our case, especially in areas that are going through a re-birth and gentrification.

On the other hand, this can also work against you. For example, this can happen if you are flipping houses and then the market crashes all of a sudden. When you enter into a flip project, a key component of your financial analysis is the after repair value—in other words, what you can sell the property for. If the market declines or worse crashes then this typically effects home sales which decline in this type of market. This has also happened to us; during the last market crash. A few single family homes that we had intended to sell ended up becoming rentals when the market crashed in 2008/2009. You always want to have multiple exit strategies.

Risk Point #2–Unforeseen renovations

Another key risk point is unforeseen required renovations outside of your budget. Even with the best plan in place, unexpected issues during the flip process can come up. You need to have a contingency in your budget (typically 10–15% of construction costs). During the renovation process of one of our flips, it was discovered that one of the walls had severe termite damage and we didn't realize it until after the budget and scope of work were created. This cost us an extra $6,000, i.e. it reduced our profit by $6,000.

Again, we can't stress it enough to always have a contingency line in your budget for these unforeseen costs.

Q: What is your favorite part about your strategy?

A: What we love about fixing and flipping homes is transforming unwanted and undesirable properties into desirable, functional homes for families to raise their children in. We love being able to not only improve a property, but as a result improve a neighborhood.

One example is a dilapidated 3-story row home that was over 100 years old that we flipped. When we bought it, the house had drugs throughout the home; it was sad to see heroin needles and children's toys right next to each other. However, after about $120,000 worth of renovations, we sold it to a young couple about to start a family.

We also really like the beginning of the project the most—creating the vision and plan for the finished product, creating the budget, and putting the team in place.

Q: Is how you do your strategy now different in any way than it was when you started? If so, how is it different?

A: We bought/sold our first fix and flip about 14 years ago. When we first got started, we figured it all out as we would go (which by no means is an effective strategy!). We did not analyze the property properly. For example, for our first flip, one of the first things we had our contractor do was replace the roof since we noticed several leaks. Well, after replacing the roof, we noticed several places of structural damage and after several discussions with various contractors, it was determined that the house was not salvageable and would need to be torn down. So the house with the brand new roof was torn down. This was super frustrating at the time. However, we learned an important lesson: always have a clear plan and budget BEFORE you begin construction! Then your goal is to execute the plan to completion.

As we've gotten more experience, we have systemized working with contractors since we began. For example, we have systemized contractor payment schedules and inspections at specific project milestones. The other growth has been focus. When we began we allowed ourselves to get pulled into tons of flip markets and over the years refined our focus and only work in specific markets where we have a team in place and yield the returns that meet our goals.

Also when we started we looked for cheap deals. As we have continued, we focus more now on first time home buyers, strong schools, low inventory of finished product, low days on market, and having team members in that local area bring our vision to a reality.

Q: What advice would you give new investors starting out in this strategy?

A: First and foremost, the process of fixing and flipping homes is not as easy as it looks on TV. While it's not rocket science, it's just not as simple as TV shows make it look.

Our advice to newbies:

- Start small to mitigate your risk. Don't get into something with a $100,000 renovation budget as your first flip (unless you're partnered with a team that knows a ton more than you do!). Make sure you walk before you run.

- Run your numbers by someone more experienced.

- Run your construction plan by someone more experienced.

- Put EVERYTHING in writing.

- Begin with the end in mind—always have a plan before you begin a project.

- Hire reputable and trustworthy contractors.

- Remember that your job is to manage timeline and the budget like a HAWK.

- In a "hot market", watch out for overpaying for a property.

- When inventory is low, watch out for overpaying for a property.

- Only buy deals in desirable areas that have strong home sales and low inventory.

- When challenges arise, learn from them, and keep the project moving to completion.

- Communicate, communicate, communicate with your team.

Investor Bio: Matt Faircloth

Matt Faircloth has been a full-time investor for 15 years. In that time he has successfully completed projects involving dozens of fix and flips, office buildings, single family homes, and apartment buildings. He started with a $30,000 private loan and has now completed over $40,000,000 in transactions involving private money. He is a regular contributor to BiggerPockets.com, has an active YouTube Channel dedicated to educating investors, and is the author of the Amazon Bestseller, *Raising Private Capital: How to Build your Real Estate Empire with Other People's Money* published by BiggerPockets.

Investor Bio: Liz Faircloth

Liz Faircloth, co-founder of the DeRosa Group, based in Trenton NJ, is an owner of commercial and residential property throughout the east coast with a mission to "transform lives through real estate." DeRosa has vast experience in bringing properties to their highest and best use, which includes repositioning single family homes, multi-family, apartment buildings, mixed-use, and office space. The company controls close to 700 units of residential and commercial assets. Liz is one of the founders of the Real Estate InvestHER Community and the co-host of "The Real Estate InvestHER Show," a podcast providing straight talk along with inspiration for existing and aspiring women real estate investors to live both balanced and financially free lives.

You can find them at:

www.derosagroup.com
www.therealestateinvesther.com

For social media links and access to free giveaways, including *The InvestHER Financial Freedom Road Map,* and membership programs, click on Matt & Liz's pictures on the *NOT Your How-To Guide to Real Estate Investing* resources site www.aliboone.com/book-goodies.

chapter twenty-two

Sharon Vornholt

Primary strategy: Wholesaling
Location: Louisville, KY
Location of investments: Louisville, KY
21 years' experience, 11 years wholesaling

Q: Can you describe your investment strategy?

A: I am a wholesaler at this time, however I have also been a re-habber and a buy-and-hold landlord. I was a rehabber and a buy and hold landlord for 10 years until the crash in 1998. That's when I became an "accidental wholesaler".

I specialize in probates, as well as marketing and branding your real estate business. Probate is the legal process of administering a deceased person's estate. This involves organizing their money, assets and possessions and distributing them as inheritance, after paying any taxes and debts. Investors provide a valuable service to these folks since they have to sell the property in the estate

Real property like houses, land, etc. must be sold to pay the cred-itors, before the heirs can get what they are inheriting. The cred-itors include anyone that is owed money like outstanding loans or mortgages, credit cards, hospital and nursing home bills, and funeral expenses.

Many times, the property in the estate is a distressed property that would need a lot of work before it could be listed on the

MLS and the heirs don't want to spend their time or money doing this. Since the property **must** be sold to settle the estate (unless it was directly inherited or part of a trust), these folks can be very motivated sellers. As a wholesaler, this is very advantageous for me in terms of where I find the properties that I wholesale.

Q: How much time do you typically spend on your investments?

A: It used to be my full-time job. I spend 25–35 hours a week currently. Today I have someone that takes care of that side of the business, so I can focus on the education side of my business. I teach investors marketing, branding and how to build a profitable probate investing business.

No two days are alike for me!

Q: Can you walk us through a typical deal?

A: The timeline: 2 weeks or less in most cases. Probates may take a little longer to close, but the process is the same.

1. *Find a deal through the marketing strategies you are using in your business.* Have 3–5 marketing channels to find deals. Take the seller calls you get from your marketing. Look at the properties you're interested in. (note: I have to know how to analyze properties so I can know which properties I'm interested in.)

2. *Make the offer to the seller.* Negotiate if necessary.

3. *Write up the contract to buy the property.*

4. *Call my buyer's list and sell the property to one of them.* Call the buyer on my list I think will want this particular property (I know my buyers).

5. *Write the contract to sell the property.*

6. *Send both contracts to my closing attorney.*

7. *Go to closing and do a double-close using none of my own money.*

8. *Pick up a big check.*

Q: What skills do you use regularly for your strategy?

A: *#1–Marketing*

Marketing is a real estate investor's number one job. If you don't have a steady stream of leads coming in the door you will be out of business in no time.

Think of it this way; if you don't have leads coming in the door you really don't need to know any of the rest of the things like building rapport with seller, negotiation etc. When it comes to probate investing, marketing to those folks is a different skill set. Your brand (which showcases your expertise) is critical to getting these sellers to choose you. They have to see you as the expert.

#2–Branding

As I said, having a strong brand makes all your marketing work better because it showcases your expertise and presents you as the expert.

> "Marketing is how you get leads.
> Branding is why they choose YOU".

When it comes to branding, your brand is how you make people feel. It's also the know, like and trust factor that you are creating with your brand. Branding is what supercharges all your marketing. Some people think branding is just colors, fonts and logos and those are certainly part of the physical aspects of your brand. However, as I said, your brand is how you make people feel. It's also what they say about you when you leave the room; whether you are trustworthy, easy to work with, whether you are the person that brings them great deals.

When it comes to branding here are some things you must do:

- You must have a website. People judge whether you are a "real business" by whether you have a professional looking website.

- You need to build a strong social media presence. This is the perfect place for people to learn about what you do.

- Creating some type of content will build trust and credibility for you and your business. Video is one of the quickest ways to build your brand whether that is through Facebook lives, or videos that you make and post on your website and social media. They don't have to be fancy. People are looking for authenticity.

- Become a networking ninja. You want people to think of you when they have a deal to sell. The only way for that to happen is for you to get out and meet people. Attend your local REIA meeting and volunteer.

#3–People skills/building rapport (problem solving)

This is a must. You have to be able to talk to sellers in a way that helps solve their problem to be successful as a real estate investor. We are really in the problem-solving business.

If you have a truly motivated seller, they have a problem or an immediate need. They may have a house in probate that they must sell in order to settle the estate. Or, they may have a situation where there is an immediate need or a financial reason they become a motivated seller. Maybe they have lost their job; they have to relocate quickly to another state; maybe they are getting a divorce or there is some other reason. Whatever that reason is, they have a problem. They have a house the must sell quickly. You are there to help solve their problem, but you always want to create a "win-win" situation for everyone involved.

I would like to point out that these are not always distressed properties. People are often willing to give up some equity for a quick sale that solves their underlying problem like a job transfer or probate property.

However, when it comes to distressed property, the numbers are the numbers. You can only offer what the property is worth no matter what their situation is. You might be able to offer them a creative solution where they get more money for the property, but you get better terms. Great deals are created not found.

#4–Negotiating

I am always negotiating directly with the seller or the executor of the estate if it's a probate since I only work off market deals. On a rare occasion I might work with an agent if it's a pocket deal.

Negotiation is always about the price and/or the terms. One way of negotiating is to go for a low, cash offer to the seller. You might also do deal where the terms of the deal are more important than the price. For example, you might pay more for a property if the sellers will do a low or no down payment deal with seller financing. This would be a "terms" deal.

If you suck at negotiation you will almost always pay too much for the property. You generally make money the day you buy the property. You will likely break even or lose money on a rehab where you have paid too much for the property initially. If you are a wholesaler, your investor buyer will quickly move on to other wholesalers if you send the bad deals.

It's important to get over your fear of negotiation. Almost everyone has this challenge in the beginning.

#5–Knowing the numbers

You can't make intelligent offers if you don't know your numbers. In order to more thoroughly understand the numbers, you have to understand how much a potential renovation is going to cost. There are no shortcuts when it comes to learning how to estimate repairs. First of all, you need a property inspection form that you use to walk through the house and note anything that needs to be repaired or replaced. Once you have determined what needs to be repaired or replaced, then you have to determine how much that will cost.

When it comes to learning how to estimate repairs, I spent a lot of time in Home Depot when I first got started. You simply must know how much materials cost. How much are cabinets? Then, how much will the installation be? When it comes to the major systems, you can get bids or have contractors give you an estimate on things like the roof, HVAC system, electrical etc. This is one of the benefits of belonging to your local REIA group. You can simply ask someone how much a furnace costs for a 1200 square foot ranch with a basement.

#6–Following up

As many as 80% of my deals come from follow-ups. FYI, often that is after someone has said "no".

Q: What are the primary risk points with your strategy? How severe is each risk point, and what are the consequences of each?

A: There really isn't much risk in wholesaling. You don't need a lot of cash or even good credit to build a successful wholesaling business.

However, you do need the ability to estimate repairs accurately and access to comps in order to make strong, accurate offers to buy property. As a wholesaler, you need to be sure your numbers are right before you present a deal to your investor buyer. You can't know what to offer on a property unless you determine how much the repairs will cost. If you pay too much for a property then present the deal to an investor buyer and the numbers are wrong, they will lose confidence in you. They won't want to work with you going forward.

Q: What is your favorite part about your strategy?

A: Wholesaling is a way to make quick chunks of cash. You can use these chunks of cash as your primary source of income, you can pay off your rentals with this money, or you can build a cash reserve for your rehabbing business. I think wholesaling should be part of every investor's business no matter what their main investing strategy is.

Probates have been my #1 source of leads for a very long time, and they are easy to wholesale. I love probates because they aren't market-driven, you will never run out of leads, and the house almost always has to be sold in order to settle the estate. These can be very motivated sellers. Wholesalers can offer these folks a quick sale for their unwanted property.

What's the downside of wholesaling? It's a job. If this is your strategy, you will want to create systems and automate as much as you can.

Q: Is how you do your strategy now different in any way than it was when you started? If so, how is it different?

A: Yes. My business is very different today than when I started. First of all, I already had a very demanding business, so I invested part-time for 10 years. I would do a rehab and then buy a rental with the cash. I went along just like that for a decade before going full-time. When the real estate crash impacted Louisville in 2008, the reality was that it was very difficult for homeowners to get a mortgage. That can be the kiss of death for a rehabber. Having to hold a property for months or maybe even a year before finding a buyer was a very scary thing.

I was always a good marketer so I was still generating a steady stream of leads. Since I didn't want to get stuck holding a house for a long time, I did a complete pivot in my business and did my first wholesale deal. I learned quickly that all I needed was just a 4–6 of the right buyers on my list; those that either had cash or still had access to cash. At the end of the day, I had a mix of landlords and rehabbers.

Over that 10 year period I built a strong network, so wholesaling became easy for me.

Q: What advice would you give new investors starting out in this strategy?

A: To succeed as a wholesaler, you have to get good at marketing, learn what a good deal looks like, and you need a buyer's list.

I can tell you what the #1 thing an investor should focus on, and that is marketing. You should have a time slot dedicated to marketing every day. I also recommend that investors have 3–5 lead channels (or ways to get deals) at all times. Those will likely be different for each investor. For instance; one investor might use direct mail, have a lead generation website, do some driving for dollars, and make it a point to get in a few networking events each month. That's four rock solid marketing strategies.

I believe direct mail should be one of every investor's marketing strategies. It's the best way for getting off market deals, and it's really the only way to effectively market to probates. One thing I know for sure is, you never want to put all your eggs in one basket. A case in point would be when REO's were plentiful a lot of investors stopped doing all their other marketing activities. Then one day, those REO leads just dried up.

You should have some cash on hand if possible—for marketing. While it's true that it's possible to start with no cash or credit, from a marketing standpoint wholesaling is so much easier to have some money for marketing. I think it should be a part of everyone's business regardless of your main marketing strategy. Think of it this way; wholesaling is a niche where you can make big chunks of cash. Landlords can use this cash to pay down their rentals, and rehabbers can build a cash reserve through wholesaling.

If you're doing a good job of marketing, you will come across a lot of houses that don't meet your particular investing criteria. These are the houses you wholesale to other investors. Where do you find those people? You find them at your local REIA.

You only need a 5–6 full time rehabbers at most to have a pipeline that will buy all your deals. You also need a couple of landlords for more marginal deals. For instance, a rehabber might want to gut a kitchen and redo the whole thing. Whereas a landlord, might simply paint the cabinets, install new flooring and call it done so their repair costs are much different.

Investor Bio: Sharon Vornholt

Sharon Vornholt is the owner of Innovative Property Solutions in Louisville, KY. She owned and operated a successful home inspection business for 17 years, while also investing part-time for over a decade. Sharon was originally a rehabber and a buy and hold landlord. When the market crashed in 2008, she became an "accidental wholesaler". That was also the time she closed her other business to focus on real estate full-time. Today her passion is in teaching other real estate investors how to succeed in this business.

Sharon is best known as a marketing and branding expert, and for her expertise in probate investing. She has helped hundreds of people refine their brand and create customized marketing plans that work.

Sharon is also the go-to person if you want to know how to succeed in one of the most lucrative niches in real estate, probates. She helps people become the "go to expert" in their area in just 6 short weeks through her course, Probate Investing Simplified.

Sharon is the creator of the Louisville Gal's Real Estate Blog and the popular podcast "Let's Talk Real Estate Investing". Sharon hosts several live events each year and is a regular speaker at other events across the country.

You can find her at:

www.LouisvilleGalsRealEstateBlog.com
www.probateinvestingsimplified.com

For social media links and access to Sharon's *Probate Investing Simplified Course* and her *Let's Talk Real Estate Investing* podcast, click on her picture on the *NOT Your How-To Guide to Real Estate Investing* resources site www.aliboone.com/book-goodies.

chapter twenty-three

Ali Boone

Primary strategy: Buy &Hold–Turnkey Rental Properties
Location: Los Angeles, CA
Location of investments: out-of-state
9 years' experience

Q: Can you describe your investment strategy?

A: I buy "turnkey rental properties", which means the rental properties are already rehabbed, tenanted, and with property managers set up to manage the property once I own it. The term "turnkey" is technically related to the condition of the property—the idea being that all you have to do is put the key in the door of the property and you're making cash flow on day one (because the rehab and all that is already done)—but when I buy turnkeys, and the turnkeys I work with, are sold through turnkey provider companies who specifically sell turnkey properties to investors. Ultimately, I shop through the turnkey inventories, choose a property I like, put it under contract, conduct due diligence on it to verify everything is as advertised, and then I close on the property. Once I close on the property, meaning I own it, the property managers take over and manage the property for me. The only time I'm ever needed is if a decision needs to be made, like for repairs or something, or if I need to make a change with the property management. Otherwise, I'm just collecting the monthly cash flow and keeping an eye on the statements.

Q: How much time do you typically spend on your investments?

A: I spend little to no time on my properties. Assuming all is going well, the only things I'm doing are occasionally approving repairs with the property management company or asking for clarifications on the statement. When this is all that's happening, I probably spend less than a cumulative hour on my properties in a year. The only times I've had things get more intensive is when I've had to hire and fire property management companies over the years, which obviously takes a little time. But even when that's happened, it's always been tasks I've been able to do over the phone and generally still doesn't take a lot of time. The only things that would ever take a significant amount of time, and even that is relative compared to other investment strategies, is if I'm buying a property and going through the due diligence and financing processes or if I wanted to oversee a major rehab due to significant tenant damage or something like that.

Q: Can you walk us through a typical deal?

A: The turnkey process is pretty straightforward, and it's the same every time I buy one.

1. *Select a market I want to invest in and the provider I want to buy through.* I need to be smart on what markets I'm buying in and what turnkey provider I'm working with, just so I can avoid headache and potential problems down the road. So I spend a little time studying up on those and working with other people in the industry to figure out where I should be buying and who I should be buying through. But once that's done initially, I don't really have to do it again for subsequent properties unless I'm changing markets or providers.

2. *Shop through the available property inventories.* This part is fun. I literally just get lists of the available properties and I shop through them and see which ones I like. The properties always have their pro forma cash flow numbers with them, pictures, neighborhood information, etc.

3. *Choose the property I like.* Once I find a property I like, I select that property either by verbally telling the provider I want it or some companies have reservation forms I fill out.

4. *Put it under contract and send in earnest money.* The provider sends over the sales contract, I sign that, send it back to them, and deposit my earnest money into escrow. The earnest money, usually $5,000, is used to hold the property and goes toward the final payment.

5. *Do due diligence to verify everything about the property.* This is the most important part of buying any property, but especially with a turnkey property because investors hear that turnkeys are "hands-off", so they think they can get away with not having to put any effort in. As an investor, it's absolutely up to me to verify exactly what I'm buying. Turnkey providers aren't perfect, properties aren't always perfect, and I don't want to have to be responsible for something that was missed during the rehab period. I want the turnkey provider to be responsible for that, so I do my due diligence to ensure everything is in working order. This includes things like the property inspection (by a licensed home inspector), verifying all of the numbers, getting information on the neighborhood the property's located in, and interviewing the property

managers who come with the property to ensure I feel good about how they operate.

6. *Close on the property.* The closing process is no different on turnkeys than with any other kind of property. My lender is usually the one who coordinates the closing with me and the provider/seller, and they have all the documents drawn up that I have to sign. With turn-keys, since they are usually purchased non-locally by the investor, it's usually assumed it will need to be a mobile notary public who can meet the investor wher-ever he or she lives to sign the paperwork.

7. *Manage the managers.* Once I close on the property, my only real job is to make sure it keeps performing. The property manager is ultimately the critical factor in whether it continues to perform or not. I never want to micromanage the property manager, but I do want to keep an eye on them and the income coming in to make sure everything seems to be running smoothly. I have had to fire property managers in the past and hire new ones. Over the years I've owned turnkeys, the fir-ing and hiring of managers has taken more of my time than anything else, but even that time is minimal and I've always been able to do it over the phone, rather than having to fly out and meet them in person.

Q: What skills do you use regularly for your strategy?

A: *#1—Decision making*

Because I'm mostly managing people rather than managing the properties directly, most of my job comes down to decision mak-ing. I'm rarely the one implementing a decision, but I am the owner of the property so ultimately it's up to me on how things are done and how they should be going. This happens first when I'm deciding on the property I want to buy, and then it's in how the property is managed. For instance, if my property manager calls me and says he got a call from a tenant about a sizeable maintenance issue, I need to be able to give some instruction or guidance on how I want the issue handled. If it's a big maintenance issue, I need to make the decision about whether to file it with insurance or not. If it's a smaller maintenance issue, I've had instances where I've been suspicious it was the tenant's fault and therefore instructed the property manager to bill the tenant directly for the work. I've also had to make the decision to fire a property manager and hire a new one when things didn't seem to be operating like they should.

Ultimately, I can't assume everyone is going to run my property perfectly or in the best way, and I have to be willing to make decisions to ensure that it is in fact running as it should, whether that's small decisions or big decisions. If I don't do that, and if I don't provide guidance on occasion, my investment is at risk.

#2–People management

My primary job as a turnkey investor is to manage the people who are carrying out the required tasks for the property. "Manage the manager", so to speak. This skill of people management really boils down to three things: knowing how to ensure I have good people in charge of those jobs (which also requires hiring and firing on occasion), knowing how I want everyone working and making sure they are all organized in such a way to support that, and being willing to put my foot down if someone isn't performing. My biggest fault over the years was not standing up to non-performing managers sooner. I would always let them convince me things will get better or that there was some viable excuse for what wasn't working. I've had to practice getting tougher with people and not letting them push me around.

#3—Due diligence/knowledge of the strategy

I have to understand enough about real estate investing principles and rental properties so that I can know if I'm buying a solid property or not. I need to be able to verify everything that is being told to me, and the only way to do that is to know what I'm looking for. What are the risk factors, what makes for a good property, what makes for a good investing market, and what things do I need to verify (via due diligence) to ensure I'm buying a property that actually is as advertised? If I don't know what I'm looking for, there's no way for me to gauge what I'm doing or what I'm being sold. Additionally, I need to understand my options and the various courses of action I can take should something go haywire. So I need to have enough knowledge about what I'm doing so that I can differentiate right from wrong and good from bad. Having and getting this knowledge may not be a skill, per say, but the willingness to study these things and gain that understanding is a required ability I have to have if I want everything to work.

Q: What are the primary risk points with your strategy? How severe is each risk point, and what are the consequences of each?

A: *Risk Point #1—Being too trusting*

The biggest risk with turnkeys is buying too far into the marketing of them that says they are "hands-off rental properties". They should be hands-off, yes, but people can take that way too literally and think they don't need to keep an eye on their property or make decisions about it. You as the owner/investor have to not only be willing to handle any challenges that arise, but sometimes the owner/investor needs to be able to identify the problems in the first place. I think that when people put all their own work into an investment property, they aren't assuming anyone else is responsible for the fate of that property. But with turnkeys, because everything is done for you, it can be tempting to assume that everything will always be taken care of on your behalf and that you don't need to participate with the property. That couldn't be more wrong. While it may be true that you have a great property manager and everything really is taken care of for you, you should never assume that will always be the case. I've always said—if there are humans in the equation, there's room for error. So always being mindful that people and things aren't always perfect, so always continue to keep an eye on things and verify things you are being told.

Risk Point #2–Property management

This isn't specific to turnkeys, but it is a factor with them because they usually come with property managers in place to manage the property once you've purchased it. Property management has a pretty bad reputation in terms of how well they tend to perform. The reality is property managers really can be terrible. It's just not a role in real estate that tends to attract the best in the business. There are some great ones out there, but it doesn't tend to be the majority. The dangerous part about bad property managers is that they can literally tank your investment if you let them. They can put bad tenants in the property who can be very costly because of extensive damages to the property and non-payment, they can falsify repair expenses which ultimately end up costing you money, they can have repairs done very poorly which ends up being costly later, etc. It's absolutely imperative you have solid property management in place or you will see your return numbers start to go down. Part of this is being willing to fire underperforming managers when it happens (notice I said "when" and not "if") and hire a new one.

Risk Point #3–General rental property risks

Turnkey is just a method of buying a rental property, not of owning a rental property. So, all the risk factors that apply to regular rental properties also apply to turnkeys. Those risks include bad tenants, unexpected property repair costs, declining locations, and declining property and rent values.

Q: What is your favorite part about your strategy?

A: The [mostly] hands-off component. I just don't want to work on my investments. If I wanted another job, I'd go get one. But aside from me not being naturally skilled at things like rehabbing or the more technical aspects that are involved in real estate investing, I would much rather spend my time doing… anything else. By taking myself out of the technical work of rental property investing, I can not only focus on the things I'm better at (in my case, project management rather than property management), but it allows me to have the capacity to grow bigger because I'm not spending all my time and energy on just one property at a time.

Q: Is how you do your strategy now different in any way than it was when you started? If so, how is it different?

A: It's really not different now than it was when I started. The only difference between now and the early days is I have a better sense of what things to look for and what due diligence to make sure I'm conducting. My biggest mistake as a newer investor was not getting rid of bad property managers soon enough. I always saw the signs, but I would talk myself out of why I needed to make a change. But in every case where there were signs, they ended up costing me money and I had to fire them and find a new one. With that said though, I'd much rather deal with property manager stress than property stress, like toilets and tenants.

Q: What advice would you give new investors starting out in this strategy?

A: Learn how to do the due diligence! As I already said, the biggest thing I've seen is people using the excuse of turnkeys being "hands-off" to not feel like they should have to put any effort into anything. There's absolutely no reason to go solely off what people tell you—there's very little about a property you can't verify on your own. So learn about the turnkey strategy, learn about rental properties, learn proper due diligence, and be able to make sound decisions.

Another important thing I would say to new investors is to not go at it alone. There are too many people in the turnkey industry who can help you for you to try to do it all yourself. There are market experts, people who specialize in vetting turnkey providers, and even fellow turnkey investors who are always willing to help. If you try to do it on your own, not only are you foregoing a lot of expertise that other people can offer you, but you also won't have support should you start to hit any challenges. The more people in your network, the more support you can have through your investing journey.

Investor Bio: Ali Boone

Ali Boone is a real estate investor and lifestyle entrepreneur and has literally defined non-conformity when it comes to her career. Ali left her corporate 9-to-5 job as an Aerospace Engineer, despite the "dream job" status that came with it, to start her real estate investing company, Hipster Investments. Hipster managed to facilitate over $18M in real estate investment transactions in it's first five years of business. Ali's primary focus in real estate, and with Hipster, revolves around passive income and passive investment options, and she is most involved with turnkey rental properties.

As of today, Ali has written over 170 articles on BiggerPockets, the world's leading real estate investing website, and she's been featured in Fox Business, The Motley Fool, Business Insider, US News, Investopedia, and Business.com. Her articles teach successful rental property fundamentals, investor psychology, and

228 Not Your How-To Guide to Real Estate Investing

strategies to help get new investors started. Her personal real estate portfolio started with buying five properties in her first 18 months of investing using only creative financing methods.

In her free time when she isn't doing real estate, she can be found skiing, volunteering in California prisons, and teaching people to fly airplanes. Her ultimate goal is to one day challenge Tim Ferriss to a lifestyle design duel.

You can find her at:

www.aliboone.com

Afterword

Are you now at the end of this book and wondering why in the world there wasn't a single how-to guide for any of the specific real estate investing strategies? If you're wondering that, you must've missed the title of the book.

This book is about mindset, which is one of the most important keys to success as a real estate investor. Long before how-to guides comes mindset. People seem to not think about this, though. Instead, they head straight for the how-to guides.

I get it. We all want to get there fast and the how-to guides seem like the quickest path. But I truly believe that if your mindset isn't right, there's not a how-to guide in the world that will help you. And this really goes for everything in life, not just real estate investing.

Since becoming an entrepreneur, I've always said that anyone can start a business. Starting it isn't the challenge; the challenge is in the roller coaster of life that comes with being an entrepreneur. Your sanity, your emotions, your bank account, and your ability to buy groceries each week will all be challenged. It's overcoming those challenges that can prove way more difficult than getting the business logistics in place. The same is true for real estate investing. It's often not the technical pieces of the industry that mess people up, but rather it's the mindset challenges that come along with it.

One of the reasons *Rich Dad Poor Dad* is such a successful book is because it introduces a mindset about money that most of us never heard growing up. Robert Kiyosaki's later books were more like how-to guides, but his initial focus with *Rich Dad Poor Dad* was about mindset. Why? Because without a change in mindset, no how-to guide can get you where you want to go.

When I first started exploring real estate investing, I was fairly clueless. I had read *Rich Dad Poor Dad* and gotten on board with that information, but there was more that I either didn't know or hadn't fully comprehended yet. For instance, I'm obviously a fan of passive income. I'm thankful *Rich Dad Poor Dad* taught me the concept of passive income, but after learning about it, I didn't know how to get it. It was only through more reading, education, and experience that I figured out ways of earning passive income. I had to piece together information, try different things, fail at things, and try some more until it began to come together. A how-to guide on how to get passive income would've been great, but it wouldn't have helped me had I not fully taken in the concept beforehand.

It's possible that some of what I've said in this book didn't resonate with you at all. At least now you know what isn't a fit for you. Knowing what's not a fit can oftentimes give you as much clarity as finding out what is a fit. At least you can probably have a better feel for which direction you should be moving in now.

Your real estate investing career will likely be as unique as you are as a person. No two people are the same, and no two real estate investing journeys will be the same. Some will be similar, but the trick to this industry is making your own path. Don't try to clone anyone else's success; it won't work. The only successful path you can create will be the one that is unique to you.

Remember, there's no award for the most independent investor who needed help from no one. Not taking or accepting help from anyone is ridiculous and accomplishes nothing. If your ego needs stroking, get the stroking someplace else that doesn't have as much of your money on the line. Real estate investing may be a solo venture, but it's very much a team sport.

And lastly, never forget the golden rule of investing: **don't lose money.** But if you do lose money, now you know that the world won't end. Just learn from it and try again.

Happy investing!

p.s. All of the concepts discussed in this book aren't just applicable to real estate investing. Consider all of them in other aspects of your life as well!

Resources

For a collection of amazing resources, go to:

www.aliboone.com/book-goodies

In this link, you will get access to:

√ The 10-Minute Plan to Financial Freedom—FREE!

√ 7 Rookie Mistakes & How to Avoid Them—FREE!

√ A downloadable calculator tool you can use to quickly run numbers on rental properties—FREE!

√ Links to connect directly with the investors interviewed and information on the programs and resources they offer

√ Articles related to topics discussed in *NOT Your How-To Guide to Real Estate Investing*

√ Recommended books that support topics discussed in *NOT Your How-To Guide to Real Estate Investing*

√ Links to connect with Ali directly

Made in the USA
Las Vegas, NV
16 April 2021